WHY DOES MY RABBIT . . . ?

WHY DOES MY RABBIT . . . ?

Anne McBride

With drawings by
Nina Bondarenko

SOUVENIR PRESS

First published 1998 by Souvenir Press Ltd,
43 Great Russell Street, London WC1B 3PA

Revised in paperback 2000

ISBN 0 285 63550 6

Typeset by Rowland Phototypesetting Ltd,
Bury St Edmunds, Suffolk

Printed in Great Britain by
Creative Print and Design Group (Wales), Ebbw Vale

To Jim, Olga, Deuce and Richard
with my love and thanks for being there

Behold, I do not give lectures or a little charity,
When I give I give myself.
WALT WHITMAN, Song of Myself

CONTENTS

APPENDICES

ACKNOWLEDGEMENTS

To Sarah Heath for suggesting I write this book. To Jim McBride, Rachel Casey, Christina Huggett, John Stokes, Paul Beech, Sue White and Julia Tubb for all their helpful comments on the early drafts of this book. To Richard Desborough for his help with proof-reading and indexing. To Henry Plotkin at University College London for letting me study rabbit behaviour under his guidance all those years ago. To Nico Preston for all his support during years of rabbit watching. To Susan Hunter, Emma Magnus and Sally Machell and many unnamed rabbit owners for their provision of innumerable anecdotes and questions about rabbit behaviour. To my mother, Olga, for all her help and food parcels. To my brother, Deuce, and my friends, especially Shelagh, for their support, and to Nina Bondarenko for giving the reader something to look at besides my prose. To my editor, Tessa Harrow, for being incredibly patient in understanding that life sometimes gets in the way of doing pleasurable things like writing books about rabbits. To all of these I say thank you. Last but not least, my thanks to Thumper, Bunny, Nomad, Pixie, Andy, Circles and all their rabbity 'friends and relations' for letting me share part of their lives.

RABBIT, RABBIT, RABBIT

Twenty years ago, in the late 1970s, this book would not have been considered for publication. While rabbits were popular, proclaimed as the ideal pet for children, people did not have much interest in what makes a rabbit tick. Rather it was regarded as a cheap animal to keep and one which required little maintenance. Indeed, many rabbits then and now spend their lives in a hutch at the bottom of the garden pretty much left on their own—often, sadly, to the detriment of their physical and psychological health. But more of that later.

Ten years ago, my first book on rabbits was published, but it is usually found in the natural history section of bookshops rather than the pet section. Why? you may ask. It is because, at that time, pet owners wanted to know what to feed their rabbit, how to breed and show it, rather than how to understand it as an animal in its own right. That was true for pet species in general and it is only in the last 15 years that we have seen pet owners show an increasing interest in the behaviour of their animals. This change in attitude was formally marked by the setting up of the Association of Pet Behaviour Counsellors in 1988. It has been accompanied by the proliferation of magazines and television programmes devoted to the antics of our furred, feathered and scaly companions.

Along with this general interest it has become increasingly accepted by owners and veterinary surgeons that problem behaviours in dogs, cats and horses can be prevented and resolved by means other than rehoming and euthanasia. More and more owners are seeking the advice of pet behaviour counsellors in order to harmonise their lives with their pets, and this has been reflected in the publication of the first three books in this series, namely John Fisher's *Why Does My Dog. . .* ? (1991), Sarah Heath's *Why Does My Cat . . .* ? (1993) and Paul McGreevy's *Why Does My Horse . . .* ? (1996).

At last it is the turn of the rabbit. This book perhaps marks the tidal wave of change in attitude and interest in the rabbit. In 1997 the first 'Vets' Day on Rabbits' was held in Britain with over 150 veterinary surgeons giving up their Saturday to learn about rabbit health and behaviour. I was pleased to have been asked to contribute to such an auspicious event. Ever more frequently, rabbits with behaviour problems are being referred to behaviour counsellors, rather than being put into rescue centres or even being euthanised. A great step forward for rabbit welfare.

Pet ownership practices have changed dramatically over the last couple of decades. For the first time, in 1995, the cat was more popular than the dog in the UK and the rabbit is now the third most popular mammalian pet. No longer merely the creature at the bottom of the garden, many rabbits share their owner's sofa and live indoors like the cat or dog. This change in attitude is partly due to our changing lifestyle.

More people live alone, or in families where all the adults are out at work. This means that while pets are popular, people do not have the same amount of time available for pet ownership. Dogs are demanding companions, requiring training, space and walks—even on cold and rainy days. They cannot be left for long hours at a time, day in and day out, and if they are they tend to develop unwanted coping strategies such as barking or chewing the furniture. Purely because of the time and effort required in successfully owning dogs, they are no longer top of the pet pops.

The cat is far less demanding, does not require training and would not thank you for offering to take it out in the wind and rain. Yet our change in circumstances has altered our expectations even of pet cats. As Sarah Heath says, 'No longer do owners accept that the cat is the creature they see at mealtimes and which disappears through the cat flap when visitors arrive.' Nowadays, we ask more from our pet cat as a companion, such as being more affectionate and not using the plant stand in the hallway as a toilet. Owners want their cat to be around, to be part of the family, to be a companion. It is becoming increasingly common (though a contentious practice) to keep cats indoors throughout their lives.

Many regard rabbits as the perfect compromise. They do well as indoor pets, and in many cases have more interesting lives indoors than in a hutch in the garden. They are not particularly demanding, yet are affectionate, furry, cute and friendly. They have habits which impinge on their owners less than dogs who roll in smelly things and cats who bring you presents of dead, or not so dead, mice. Some rabbit habits, though, such as eating their own faeces, can also be considered fairly disgusting; it really depends on your personal point of view.

As a child, I had the pleasure of owning rabbits, kept in spacious combination hutch-runs. They were companions from when I was seven to when I was 21. They all lived for at least seven years and one, called Nomad because of his escapologist tendencies, reached the age of 11. I looked after the school rabbits for several years, including the logging of breeding records and coat colour which were used to help us learn about the intricacies of genetic inheritance. In case you are concerned, there was never any problem finding homes for the offspring. This early rabbity involvement was surely the influence responsible for my study of the behaviour of the domestic rabbit for my doctorate: many, many hours spent watching tapes of rabbits, recorded day and night for months at a time, as well as sharing my flat with a New Zealand White house rabbit. As with all PhDs, it was certainly hard and, to a large extent, solitary work. However, being able to spend the time studying a species very closely is a privilege. I am also privileged in that I can now put that knowledge to use in helping owners of rabbits understand their needs and their behaviour, and where necessary resolving behaviour problems. Yes, rabbits too have behaviours which can be problematic to their owners. They may be wonderful but they are not perfect. But then nor are we.

Part One

BEHAVIOUR COUNSELLING FOR RABBITS

1

BEHAVIOUR COUNSELLING FOR RABBITS?

Pet behaviour counselling, or clinical animal behaviour, is slowly but surely losing its image of an eccentric person talking to an animal lying on a couch, sharing its innermost thoughts of puppy- or kittenhood. Rather it is becoming a recognised component of the animal health service offered by the veterinary profession. The majority of behaviour counsellors are not themselves veterinary surgeons but act as a complement to the veterinary profession, much in the same way as osteopaths and physiotherapists complement human medicine as offered by the general practitioner. Areas of specialisation are becoming increasingly important as we discover more ways of maintaining our pets in good physical and psychological health.

It is important that behaviour counsellors, being complementary, work with veterinary surgeons and see animals only on referral. There may be an underlying physical disease or injury involved in the behaviour problem. The Association of Pet Behaviour Counsellors (APBC) requires that their members only see animals on referral. The APBC has an extensive network of members both in Britain and abroad. This means that if an individual counsellor (who may not be a rabbit specialist) cannot help you, he or she will be able to put you in contact with someone who can.

Pet behaviour counselling has, to date, been applied particularly to dogs and cats, and to some extent to horses.

This is partly because problem behaviour in dogs, cats and horses can have quite an impact on the owner's life. For example, if the pet is an aggressive horse, a cat that urinates indoors or a dog that destroys the furniture when left alone, the owner–pet relationship will soon start to erode. Behaviour problems in other pet species tend not to be as intrusive to the owner and may not even be considered a problem; extensive bar gnawing in hamsters or rabbits, for example, may be seen as 'normal' behaviour rather than an issue of concern.

Traditionally, where a problem is damaging the owner–pet relationship, such as the biting bunny, the animal is just judged a 'bad one' for which there is no hope of change and the problem is swiftly 'resolved' by rehoming or euthanasia. Yet rabbits and all other species we keep as pets can and do show problem behaviours which can be resolved. What is required is a good grounding in the relevant areas of science and a practical application of this to the individual animal's situation. It sounds simple, but animals are complex creatures and we are gradually extending our knowledge of them, us and our mutual relationships. How behaviour problems in animals develop and how they can be resolved is a specialist and rapidly developing subject of study. I find it both fascinating and rewarding that every day I can learn something new and have the opportunity to apply what I know to good effect.

Clinical animal behaviour draws on a variety of disciplines including veterinary science, biology, zoology and psychology. Psychologists study human and animal behaviour. Many psychologists have dedicated their lives to understanding how animals learn and think, and their contribution to both the field of animal training and to the resolution of behaviour problems is invaluable. Much of the work of these investigators, known as comparative psychologists, has involved the co-operation of many species of animal we keep as pets: cats, dogs, rabbits, as well as the psychologist's ubiquitous friend, the domestic rat. Rats are intelligent, friendly creatures and some of them taught me as a student (several decades ago) how to apply the principles of learning theory (training) without the help of check chain, lead or any other device we use on dogs. What I learnt from the rats can be and has been applied to training all sorts of animals including goldfish, dogs, cats and, of course, rabbits.

The rabbit is not the 'Dumb Wabbit' as Elmer of *Bugs Bunny* fame used to think. Psychologists have shown that it is capable of learning all sorts of things. Ethologists, comparative psychologists and biologists have studied intensively both wild and domestic rabbit behaviour. They have shown the rabbit to be a species with a complex social life and an extensive range of communication signals. It can rabbit on for hours!

The rabbit, its biology and behaviour, is poorly understood by the majority of owners and this can lead to all sorts of problems. Some, such as overgrown teeth, are physically based, others are purely behavioural. The rabbit who turns aggressive is more likely to be deemed to have gone 'mad and bad' than to be seen as fearful or territorial or even sexually aroused.

While the rabbit is often regarded as the ideal pet for children, it has been pretty low on the list of priorities in terms of veterinary care. Indeed, until recently there was little that a non-specialist veterinary surgeon could do for a rabbit. Rabbit medicine did not comprise much of the veterinary student's curriculum. This is beginning to change as the popularity of rabbits increases. Over 1.4 million are kept as pets in the UK.

The resolution of rabbit behaviour problems is still, however, a minority interest—rescue societies are inundated with unwanted pet rabbits. Records of the number of rabbits put to sleep because of behaviour problems are scarce, but a survey conducted in 1995 indicated that 16,000 rabbits were given up to UK rescue centres. In

1997 a survey of 200 UK rescue centres, conducted by Morwen Abbott of one known as 'Cottontails', showed that this number had increased to 24,000, a rise of 30 per cent in just two years. This is very depressing to us rabbit-lovers as, given the appropriate knowledge, most behaviour problems can be prevented or resolved. I hope this book contributes to the spreading of that knowledge and the engenderment of long and happy relations between rabbits and people.

2

THE HISTORY OF THE DOMESTIC RABBIT

The domestic rabbit is a direct descendant of the wild European rabbit. They are so closely related that they are still considered the same species. Both wild and domestic rabbits are officially known as *Oryctolagus cuniculus*, which literally means 'hare-like digger of underground passages'. That seems to me a pretty good description of the rabbits we know and love.

The natural homeland of the rabbit is the Iberian Peninsula, modern Spain and Portugal. When the Phoenicians discovered this area, and thus the rabbit, over 3,000 years ago, they were amazed by the number of rabbits they saw. So much so that they named the country I-shepham-im, meaning 'the land of the rabbit'. This translates in Latin to Hispania or what we call Spain.

Little else was recorded about rabbits for over a thousand years, until Pliny the Elder (AD 23–79) first noted the extensive damage that rabbits can and do cause to arable crops. He wrote, 'There is also a species of hare, in Spain, which is called cuniculus; it is extremely prolific, and produces famine in the Balearic islands, by destroying the harvests.' Wild rabbits can still do enormous amounts of damage to crops, though this has been tackled with great effect by the introduction of pest controls such as Myxomatosis and Viral Haemorrhagic Disease. Modern visitors to Majorca, Menorca and Ibiza are unlikely to see or suffer from famine because of the ravages of rabbit damage.

About 80 years before Pliny the Elder's advice to pro-spective tourists to the Balearics, Varro wrote a book on farming called *De Re Rustica* (36 BC). In this he states that Romans farmed rabbits for meat. They kept them in warrens, often putting them in cages for fattening. Keep-ing, and probably breeding rabbits in cages, rather than just as captive populations in warrens, seems then to have begun some 2,000 years ago. This can be considered as the start of the process of domestication of the rabbit, a process which continues to this day with the development of new breeds.

We know that the Romans introduced the brown hare to Britain, but it is not known if they brought rabbits as well. If they did, then the rabbits did not survive for long. The rabbit was first successfully introduced to Britain by the invading Normans, the first written record of their presence dating from 1176. It is quite likely that these furry Norman invaders of the British countryside were in fact from domesticated stock. The rabbit had been spread throughout continental Europe by man, either for the ever popular sport of hunting or by medieval monks. A papal decree of around the fifth century had stated that unborn or newly born rabbits were not considered meat and thus could be eaten during Lent.

By the sixth century the monks were experimenting with breeding for size and colour. A painting by Titian (*c.*1530) shows a pure white rabbit sitting with the Madonna. The popularity of rabbits for food and for sport also influenced the breeding of dogs. Elizabeth I used to enjoy hunting rabbits and did so with the assistance of miniature beagles called 'pocket' or 'rabbit' beagles.

Until the nineteenth century little further progress was made in the domestication of the rabbit, though many millions of rabbits were killed for their meat and fur. The spur for further domestication arose with the Industrial Revolution, when people migrated from the countryside to the rapidly expanding towns and cities with their rows of terraced houses and opportunities of employment in their dismal factories and mills.

In people's small backyards there was limited room to keep livestock other than rabbits and pigeons, both of which could be used for food. Soon friendly competitions started for the best, prettiest or other favoured characteristic. These were the beginnings of pigeon racing and pigeon and rabbit fancier clubs. Before 1850 fancy rabbits were usually patterned in some way, an early recognised breed being the English Butterfly, so called because of its butterfly-shaped smut of dark fur on its nose. However, the real stars of the shows were the Lop breeds with their elongated ears. A leading rabbit fancier, Delamer, wrote in 1854 that 'Flat Lops are the most unnatural, and therefore the most perfect and valuable rabbits in a fancier's estimation.' They remain just as unnatural looking and just as popular. Though I have to say that my personal preference is for a rabbit which looks like its wild cousins in all but colour.

THE MODERN DOMESTIC RABBIT

Domestic rabbits come in a bewildering variety of shapes, colours and sizes. The long-limbed, long-eared, rangy and aptly named Belgian Hare is in stark contrast to the Netherland Dwarf with its toy-like proportions and tiny ears. The trailing, almost immovable ears of the Lops, in some breeds dragging on the ground, are a caricature of the highly mobile ears of their wild cousins or upright-eared domestic counterparts. Fur length varies along a continuum from the short-coated Satins and the velvety texture of the Rexes to the powder-puff appearance of the Angora. Thankfully, unlike the dog world, no one has yet developed a hairless breed of rabbit. As for colour, almost anything that takes your fancy will be available in the rabbit fancy world. Coats of pure white, jet black, browns, greys, blues, silver, champagne, spotted, belted, multicoloured or even the natural-coloured, wild-type Agouti can all be found.

Apart from a few early types, bred for meat and fur, the majority of rabbit breeds are as much a statement of man's creative instincts as are paintings in the Tate. While this may have beneficial effects for the psyche of man, it may not always have been to the benefit of the rabbit. Unfortunately, unlike paintings, rabbits are living, sentient beings which require more care and consideration than inanimate works of art.

Ear and fur type can lead to problems in behaviour which are rooted in mistakes of husbandry. Lop breeds are more prone to canker, a condition caused by an infestation of ear mites. Their folded down ears provide a protected, warm moist environment in which these mites thrive. Sadly for many rabbits the infection is not detected until it is well established. Even before then the rabbit may have been given up, due to its becoming bad-tempered. I think I would tend to bad temper too, if I had sore, mite-infected ears. Another potential ear problem is sunburn, particularly for those animals with white ears.

Similar husbandry problems affect rabbits with long coats, the extremes being the Cashmeres and the Angoras. The coats on these animals require daily attention if they, and their temper, are not to suffer. The fur quickly becomes tangled and matted and grooming can be a painful experience. If left, the matted balls that develop can become so tangled that they pull on the animal's skin as it moves around. Tangles under the chin may even prevent the animal from eating or attempting to groom itself. Angoras and other long-haired breeds are extremely pretty; they embody the 'fluffy bunny toy'. But unless you really do plan to be the dedicated owner, every day for the many years your rabbit should live, please do not consider owning such breeds.

With respect to its physical characteristics, the rabbit has changed substantially through the process of domestication. This process continues as we develop new breeds such as the Miniature Rex, first recognised only in 1990. The behaviour of the rabbit, however, has not changed so radically from that of its wild forebears.

3

WHAT AFFECTS BEHAVIOUR?

Behaviour is affected by two groups of factors, those we inherit and those which influence us during the course of our lifetime. The former have been classed under the heading 'nature' and the latter under 'nurture'. For many years the scientific community debated how much behaviour was purely attributable to an animal's nature and how much due to what had occurred during its lifetime. This was known as the 'nature–nurture debate'. Until quite recently animals' behaviour was thought to be driven purely by instinct; if it was undesirable then it was unlikely to be rectifiable. We now know, however, that behaviour is the result of both genetic make-up and experiences.

This interaction between genetic and environmental factors occurs naturally and is known as natural selection. It is the means by which species evolve and change. But the genetic make-up of animals can also be influenced by man. For thousands of years certain animals have been bred selectively in order to develop bloodlines which will breed true for particular characteristics. This is known as artificial selection and it is how we have developed all the different breeds we see in, for example, dogs, cattle and rabbits.

Twentieth-century technology has allowed us to be even more influential in choosing which animal's genetic material will be used to produce the next generation. The development of artificial insemination has overcome the problem of two animals not 'fancying' each other and refusing to mate and conceive. The rapid developments in the field of transgenics in the last decade and the birth of Dolly the cloned sheep in 1997 open up ever more possible ways in which man can influence the genetics, for good or bad, of the animal and plant world.

NATURE—THE EFFECTS OF INHERITANCE

Rabbits, like people, are individuals. Unless you happen to be an identical twin then you are genetically unique. All mammals (unless cloned) inherit half their genetic make-up from their mother and half from their father. If we continue with the human analogy for a moment, we are all of the same species *Homo sapiens,* though we also come in different 'types' such as Asian and Caucasian. Types also occur in other animals, such as the warm-blooded and cold-blooded types of horse referred to by Paul McGreevy in *Why Does My Horse . . . ?* Types are the result of natural selection pressures such as climate acting on the species to improve the chances of the survival and successful reproduction of the animals in the area.

The domestic rabbit is descended from a single species of the rabbit family, the European rabbit. This evolved in a restricted area of southern Europe and was not exposed to radically different environments. Thus only one type existed. This provided the raw material for man to domesticate and change to suit his requirements.

Through artificial selection we have developed a range of different groups of rabbits which breed true for characteristics such as coat length, size and ear shape. These are known as breeds, and, in Europe, there are currently nearly 200 different breeds with a multitude of colour varieties. Sixty-one breeds are recognised in the UK by the British Rabbit Council, with over 500 colour varieties available. Most breeds of rabbit have been developed in the last 150 years. In 1850 there were ten breeds in the

UK, by 1900 this had only increased by one; by 1950 there were 32 recognised breeds and by 1995, 61.

An animal's behaviour will be determined in part by its genetic make-up. This may be a fairly direct influence; some breeds such as the Netherland Dwarf are more reactive or flighty than their more phlegmatic cousins the French Lop. But genetics also can have an indirect relationship to behaviour. In general terms, breeding for dwarfism or giantism will produce potential behaviour problems related to the physical extremes selected. Dwarf breeds, be they rabbits or dogs, tend to suffer from several problems. Of particular importance is overcrowding of teeth. The miniaturised head and mouth in the dwarf rabbit breeds mean that the continuously growing teeth are more likely to become misshapen and result in physical distress which in turn may cause changes in behaviour.

Genetics are also responsible for gender. It is perhaps obvious that males are different from females. Both have certain behaviours designed to attract the opposite sex in order to mate and ensure that their genes are passed on to the next generation. Mating, parenting and territorial behaviours are to a large extent genetically determined. These are often mediated by changes in hormone levels. The hormones of both males and female rabbits are influenced by the increasing day length, around the end of January. A part of the brain, called the hypothalamus, is alerted by messages noting the increasing ratio of light to dark as these early spring days get longer. The hypothalamus then sends hormonal messages to the sexual organs to spur them into action. Throughout the winter period the testes of the male are withdrawn into the body and non-functional. The messages from the hypothalamus cause the testes to descend and expand, reaching in wild rabbits a size of 3.0×0.8 cm ($1\frac{3}{16} \times \frac{5}{16}$ in), and to start producing spermatozoa. The female too starts to become reproductively active, entering a state of continuous oestrus, and coming into 'heat', when she is willing to be mated, for two or three days every week. The breeding season lasts from late January to the end of July. It is accompanied by behavioural changes such as increased territorial behaviour. Those of you who have noticed that your rabbit seems to be particularly grumpy when you go to get it out of its hutch in the summer may have put it down to it being hot and bothered. That may be part of the problem, but it could also just be 'the time of the year'.

NURTURE—THE EFFECTS OF THE ENVIRONMENT

Experience

All animals learn continuously throughout their lives. They learn from their experience whether stimuli they encounter are likely to have good or bad outcomes. This is called association learning. Basically it means that animals make associations between things they encounter in their world, sights, sounds, smells, and whether these have pleasant or unpleasant results. Your rabbit will quickly learn that the rattle of food being poured into its bowl is a 'good sound' and will come to you. However, if your rabbit has had the misfortune to be grabbed too enthusiastically by a child, the sound of children's voices may cause it to run into its hutch. This may be more likely with the small breeds whose bones are smaller, more fragile and not so well padded as in larger breeds.

Though animals learn throughout their lives, they tend to be more curious and learn more easily when they are young. This is true for people too: as we get older learning new skills and languages becomes harder. Early experiences can also influence an animal's attitude in later life. Gentle early handling can result in a rabbit who is more relaxed and friendly to people, though even this is not as simple as it sounds. A young rabbit who only experiences handling by women may be frightened of men later on.

It is important for all animals to remember stimuli which indicate potential danger. This is possibly even more important for a prey animal like the rabbit, where a mistake can prove fatal and the rabbit ends up as someone's dinner. As a consequence a rabbit may only need one bad experience to make an association which is difficult to change. Of course, this means that rabbits can remember. A good memory is not something we normally attribute to rabbits, but their ability to learn and remember what they have learnt has been the focus of much study in laboratories and is well documented in the literature on animal learning.

Many of you may have taught your rabbit tricks and will know it can remember what to do for a piece of apple. You can also do some learning tests to investigate your pet's feats of memory. You can teach your rabbit to distinguish between pairs of patterns in order to win a favourite titbit (pieces of Ritz crackers in the case of my house rabbit, Andy). Once he has learnt one pair of patterns, teach him another. Then give him a break of a few days or a week and see how much he remembers. Rabbits can also learn to negotiate their way around mazes in order to find a tasty morsel. In fact they are very good at this, but then in the wild they do live in underground mazes called warrens.

MANAGEMENT

Management refers to the way in which we keep animals. Domestic rabbits have a lifestyle quite different from the environment in which their ancestors evolved. They are not necessarily given the same freedom of movement, choice of sun or shade, of being above or below ground, of what to eat or who to interact with.

Rabbits can make unlikely friendships.

Companionship

The majority of rabbits spend their lives in a hutch, often without a run, with no other rabbit companion. Even if several rabbits are kept, it is likely they will be in separate hutches being able only to smell and hear their neighbours, not even seeing those living in the hutch above or below their own. They cannot choose who they are next to, and may not even like their neighbour. Even if they do they cannot groom each other or lie down next to each other in friendly companionship.

It is often advised that rabbits should be kept alone, and indeed rabbit fights can prove fatal. However, rabbits are social animals, as many a walk in the country will testify. Rabbits which are introduced to each other, preferably at an early age, around six weeks, and of similar-sized breeds, can form strong relationships. In order to avoid any fighting due to hormonal changes when they reach adulthood (and during the breeding season) it is advisable to castrate males and spay females early on.

Rabbits can also live happily with other species, such as guinea-pigs (properly known as cavies). Again introductions are best done when the animals are young. Whether your rabbit's companion is another rabbit or a cavy, it is important that enough space is provided and that there are 'escape boxes—if with a cavy, one needs to be small enough to allow the cavy in and not the rabbit. Just as with people who live together in the same house, the odd squabble between your rabbit and its companion is inevitable and provision of escape boxes can allow them to choose to separate for a while till their mood is better.

Rabbits can make unlikely friendships. House rabbits can become accepted by, and accept, what ought to be a feared foe, namely a cat or dog. Gump, a house rabbit of my acquaintance, is firm friends with Bags, the large Gordon Setter with which he lives. He is also happy to rub noses and lie down with my own Collie cross when we go to visit, and merely retreats out of the way when the two dogs start to play. Gump was introduced, carefully, to the household when both dogs were adult and there has been no problem, even though both dogs will happily chase wild rabbits given any opportunity.

Space

I am constantly dismayed by the rabbit hutches I see for sale: they are so small. This of course stems from the perception that rabbits do not need space and can live contentedly in a small hutch in the garden. *Wrong!* Rabbits, given the opportunity, will frolic, leap and run around; they are immensely curious animals. Being cooped up in a hutch for years on end can result in physical and psychological damage. On top of this, there is little regard for differences in rabbit size. So called 'starter rabbit hutches' are advertised in many pet shops. These *may* be suitable for baby rabbits, or even adults of dwarf breeds, though without a run attached I think not. In any case, baby rabbits grow and the hutch that was large enough for them to lie out flat or stretch to their full height when a baby may not be big enough for them to do so when they are adult. Many rabbits only have space to hop a pace or two from one end of their hutch to the other. Not the way I would like to spend my life!

Lack of room means that rabbits can develop deformed spines, which can be extremely painful, particularly when the rabbit is picked up and handled. This in turn may cause a rabbit to become aggressive as it associates being picked up with back pain. Lack of exercise means that rabbits suffer from osteoporosis or weak bones. This makes them more susceptible to fractures, particularly in the larger breeds. Lack of exercise also means the rabbit is likely to become overweight, have a weak heart and a shorter life. Not what anyone would wish for their pet.

An integrated hutch and run system allows the rabbit to choose to be out or in, to run or sit, to be in sun or shade. Such a system needs to be large enough to allow the animal to run, hop, jump and stretch. It also needs to be escape proof, with a lid and wire bottom to deter digging out, as well as fox and cat proof. This way your rabbit can be physically more healthy and a happy, more entertaining pet.

Diet
The saying that we are what we eat is as true for rabbits as it is for people. What we eat affects our health and can affect our behaviour.

The rabbit is an efficient eater with a gut based on the system of recycling, that is they use everything twice to get the maximum benefit. Rabbits and other members of the family *Lagomorpha* (hares and pikas, the rock-rabbits of the Americas) are unique in the animal kingdom in terms of their digestion. Food processing in this group has reached a pinnacle of efficiency.

Rabbits evolved in a habitat characterised by low-quality scrubland and their digestive system has evolved to extract the maximum amount of goodness from food low in nutrient and calorific value. Rabbits pass their food right through their gut twice. In order to do this a rabbit indulges a peculiar habit known as refection. Using its mouth it catches some of its faecal droppings straight from the anus and then swallows them. Ugh! The droppings you find on the bottom of your rabbit's hutch are hard and dry and contain the residues of food which the rabbit cannot use. The droppings it catches and swallows are soft, moist and covered in mucus. This second trip of the food through the gut is when most of the absorption of nutrients takes place. What is left is what you see and clear up.

This system is efficient not only because it allows rabbits to live on low-quality feed, but also because it means they do not have to spend long above ground where they are exposed to predators. Instead they can fill their bellies and then retire to the safety of the warren to continue the bulk of the digestive process. The soft droppings are produced during the day when they are resting below ground or in the middle of the night when they tend not to be grazing.

In domestic situations people are inclined to feed their rabbits on commercial, pelleted rabbit food, often a mixture of pellets and flakes made from grasses, oats, bran, peas and corn. These are much more nutritious than the grasses found in their native habitat. In addition such concentrated food does not take them so long to eat, nor do they necessarily get a balanced diet as, like the rest of us, they will choose to eat the tasty bits in preference to all of the food in the bowl.

Such high-quality food, and possibly unbalanced diet, can affect a rabbit's behaviour. It can be responsible for increasing a tendency for aggression, particularly if the rabbit has little else to occupy its time. It is rather like feeding a racehorse full of oats but not allowing it to run, or feeding a boxer lots of steak and eggs but not allowing him to fight it off.

Another problem with pelleted food is that it does not allow the rabbit to use its teeth in the way for which they have evolved. Rabbit teeth are designed for slicing and, particularly, grinding. Small, hard pellets of food cannot be sliced but require crushing by the molars (see Anorexia, p. 92). This in turn can lead to misalignment of the teeth. This problem is exacerbated by the high level of nutrition of the food, which makes the teeth grow more rapidly than they can be worn down. Misaligned teeth become pathologically long and a common remedy is to have them clipped by the vet. This in itself can result in fracture of the teeth, so causing further misalignment. It is also likely to be painful, as anyone who has had a broken tooth will agree.

The real answer is to ensure that the bulk of your rabbit's diet is in the form of hay (dried grasses), green plants and items such as carrots and dandelions. This will give the rabbit a balanced diet, good for its teeth, and provide it with a natural way to occupy its time.

It was interesting to note that at the first conference on rabbit health, experts in rabbit teeth, respiratory problems and behaviour all had a single common message: *rabbits are designed to eat grass.*

KNOW THE BEAST

In order to understand the behaviour of modern domestic rabbits we need to look at their history. History affects an animal in two ways: the ancestral history of the species, its evolution, and the personal history of the individual, its life experiences. Many of the behaviours we shall consider in the next part, Wild Rabbit, Domestic Rabbit, will be species-typical and have arisen from the rabbit's evolutionary history. In the final part, Why Does My Rabbit . . . ?, many of the behaviours discussed will be influenced by the experience of the individual.

This splitting of the causes of behaviour into those stemming from the species' or the individual's history is applicable to all animals, including ourselves. In truth the split is not clear cut: the behaviour an individual produces in response to particular experiences will be rooted in that individual's genetic blueprint, which in turn is rooted in its family history, which in turn is rooted in the species' evolutionary history.

The modern rabbit originated in the dry, Mediterranean climate of southern Spain. Its ancestors had retreated there to escape the coldness of the Ice Age. Not so different from those of us who retreat to warmer climes to escape the British winter, but there any similarity ends.

Perhaps the most important clue to understanding the rabbit is that it is a prey animal with a lot of enemies. Wild rabbits weigh about 1.5 kg (3 lb 4 oz) and are considered a medium-sized prey item. That is, they provide a more satisfying meal than shrews or mice, and are small enough to be caught by an animal working on its own—unlike, say, a wild zebra which needs two or more lions to bring it down.

Wild rabbits are high on the menu of over 20 different species of predator. They have enemies which attack them from above, including buzzards, owls and even golden eagles. They are chased and caught by foxes which, like badgers, will also dig baby rabbits from their nest burrows. Even adult rabbits are not safe underground. Stoats and weasels are perhaps their worst enemies. Marauding family groups of these animals hunt rabbits in an organised fashion. Some members of the hunting party descend into the warren chasing the terrified inmates to the surface, where they are caught by the rest of the group waiting at the exit holes. It was not for nothing that Kenneth Grahame portrayed the stoats and weasels as the 'baddies' in *The Wind in the Willows*.

The main requirements for a full and productive life are to have enough to eat, to avoid being eaten and to reproduce. The majority of the behaviour of animals is orientated towards fulfilling these three aspects of existence. As we will see later, much of the rabbit's behaviour is geared to avoiding being eaten and ensuring the survival of the young. Even the process of refection, described in the section on diet above, is designed to reduce the chances of a rabbit falling foul of a predator.

The recognition that the rabbit is a prey species has far-reaching implications in explaining why rabbits do what they do and how we should treat them. In general terms, the communication of prey species is more restricted and subtle than that of predator species, such as the dog. The process of evolution has selected against rabbits showing extravagant signs of greeting, pain or fear. Such displays can be fatally costly as they can draw attention to the signaller and may indicate that the individual is in some way vulnerable and thus an easy target, even if only because it is so busy greeting its fellows that it is not paying attention to the possible presence of a predator nearby.

The primary concern of those involved in the domestication of the rabbit, from the early monks to the modern rabbit fancier, has been to produce rabbits with different physical characteristics. Altering their behavioural traits has not been a principal aim. This is the opposite of what happened in the case of the dog, where man has artificially selected for particular behavioural traits such as a strong herding instinct in sheepdogs, a strong territorial instinct in the guard breeds or a strong fighting instinct in the terriers. As a consequence it is less easy to extrapolate directly from the behaviour of the domestic dog's ancestor, the wolf, to the behaviour of the dogs we see today. Studies have shown, however, that the behaviour of wild and domestic rabbits is very similar. This justifies us in relating the behaviour we see in domestic rabbits to what we know of the behaviour and habitat of their wild cousins.

Part Two

WHAT IS A RABBIT?

4

WILD RABBIT, DOMESTIC RABBIT

In this part of the book, I will attempt to highlight the basic features of wild rabbit behaviour. You may well smile as you recognise characteristics of your own rabbit's behaviour in the following descriptions, and gain a better understanding of why your rabbit does what it does.

A TO Z OF WILD RABBIT BEHAVIOUR

Alertness

The possibility of being someone's meal pervades all aspects of the rabbit's existence and being alert is its first line of defence, a constant activity that requires the use of all the rabbit's highly developed senses of smell, hearing and sight. Of the three senses, smell is probably the most important.

Rabbits spend much of their time in the dark, underground during most of the day, coming to the surface at dusk and retreating below ground soon after dawn. Even when a rabbit is apparently asleep, dozing in the late afternoon sun, its nose will be continually surveying the area for the slightest hint of danger carried on the air. The rabbit's nose is a lifeline in two ways. Not only is it the main route for air entering the lungs, but it is its principal radar, early warning system. The wild rabbit who succumbs to an infection which harms its sense of smell is unlikely to last long. For me as a child the twitch, twitch, twitch of the nose was such a prominent characteristic of rabbits that my first rabbit went by the full name of Thumper Whiffly McBride, 'to whiffle' meaning to blow in puffs or slight gusts. The movement of the nose draws air into the nostrils. As the air is drawn in, the rabbit's split top lip parts to expose the moist underside, this moistness enhancing the strength of any scent passing over it. Many of the chemicals which produce a particular smell may be mixed with water, making them more easily detected by the nerve-endings inside the nasal passage. This relationship between water, scent molecules and nasal nerves explains why flowers in our garden smell stronger after a light rain or in the early morning and evening when they are covered in dew.

Perhaps the parts of the body which first come to mind when we think of a rabbit are its ears. They are so ridiculously large compared to the small neatly rounded head they adorn. This large surface area enables the rabbit to funnel more sound waves into the ear itself and thereby detect noises of very low volume. A rabbit can manoeuvre its ears independently of each other, rather like a horse, allowing the animal to detect sound from more than one direction at once and to pinpoint the source accurately.

The third aspect of the rabbit radar system is its eyesight. The eyes bulge and sit prominently at the sides of the head near the top. This position gives a wide field of vision, almost completely around the body. In fact, the area the rabbit is least able to see is directly in front of it. However, with its nose and ears allowing it to locate the direction of any potential danger, the rabbit can then turn its head to assess the situation.

As any military commander would agree, the more eyes, the better the chances of detecting a sneaky attack by the enemy. This is probably the main reason why rabbits live in groups. The greater the number of rabbits on the surface, the more eyes, ears and noses there are to spot any predator and the higher the chances of any single individual having enough warning to make a successful escape.

Vigilance comprises a major part of a rabbit's feeding activity. Grazing is frequently interrupted by brief scans of the area. You may have noticed your own rabbit taking a mouthful of food and then, while chewing, lifting its head or even sitting bolt upright on its back legs in order to get a better view. In my own studies of domestic rabbits I found that about 12 per cent of the rabbit's behavioural repertoire is spent sitting up in this alert position. It spends considerably longer sitting or lying down, some 60 per cent of the time, perhaps digesting its food, but all the while its ears, eyes and nose are 'on alert'. Some other rabbit studies have shown that the frequency with which a rabbit interrupts its feeding depends on both how many other rabbits are around and how far an individual rabbit is from its burrow. The more rabbits about, the less time any single individual spends scanning the horizon. Individual scanning episodes may comprise several short checks, known as 'spotting', or longer vigilance episodes, known as 'studying'.

The relationship between where a rabbit is feeding and how vigilant it is is rather more complicated. If feeding close to a place where a predator could be hiding, near a hedgerow or a shed in the garden, for instance, then the rabbit will lift its head often to check that all is well, a lesson Peter Rabbit's father had not learnt, to his cost. Frequent checking is also necessary if the animal is feeding a long way from its burrow, at a distance of over 35 metres (38 yards). To cover this sort of distance at speed is quite an effort and may mean it gets outrun and caught by a swift-footed foe such as a fox. But when the rabbit is feeding a reasonable distance from its burrow and clear of any cover which could be advantageous to an enemy, it can afford to relax a little, knowing it has time to retreat to its burrow if surprised. If you carry your own rabbit to an outside run during the day, it is worth ensuring there is a box or small hutch in the run. Apart from the obvious advantage of providing shade from the sun or shelter from the rain, such cover will allow your pet to feel safer and more relaxed while it mows the grass for you.

Predator detection is not the only function of vigilance. It has been found that how far a rabbit is from its mate will also affect its level of alertness. The further the female is away from the male, and vice versa, the more often checks are made on the other's position and activity . . . rather like us.

Breeding

Being alert means a rabbit is likely to survive while it is getting enough to eat. It can then get on with the real business of living, namely reproduction. Breeding and rearing offspring successfully enables an animal to pass on its genetic material, its genes, to the next generation. Rabbits are notorious for their ability to breed; in fact they 'breed like rabbits'.

The breeding season is determined by day length and in Britain starts in January and ends in late July. The first litters are born in early February. In a good season a single doe can produce six litters, a total of 30 young a year. Pregnancy lasts for 30–31 days and a female is able to be mated within 12 hours of giving birth. Thus, apart from the first and last litters of the year, a female is likely to be spending spring and summer pregnant with one litter, while nursing another.

Of course, for one reason or another, not all pregnancies reach full-term. Unlike many mammals, including humans, rabbits do not abort foetuses which have not survived, but reabsorb them through the uterus. This is an adaptive solution to the rabbit's problem of survival in its native habitat. Reabsorption means that the female does not waste all the energy she has spent on developing the foetus inside her body. Also, by not aborting the foetus she does not leave any easy pickings for predators.

Infant rabbits are called kittens, too.

The majority of foetuses do, however, survive. Some four weeks after conception, they come into the world, blind, deaf and hairless, but with the ability to smell. In less than a month they are weaned and left to fend for themselves amongst the rest of the colony, while their mother gets on with the business of rearing the next litter.

Rabbit kittens grow extremely fast. By 18 days of age they are furred, with fully functional ears and eyes, and weigh five times the amount they did at birth. By the time they are four months old, rabbits are sexually mature, though they do not reach full adult size until nine months. Young males therefore find it difficult to compete with fully grown adult males for access to females. In contrast, young females which are born early in the season are likely to have babies of their own later that same season. So not only could our original mother rabbit have produced some 30 young in a year, but some of those may well have given her grandchildren as well. No wonder rabbits have such a reputation for their breeding ability.

On this basis you might expect to find the countryside knee-deep in rabbits, which it clearly is not. Rabbits in the wild suffer high rates of mortality. Young and old are likely to become items on someone's menu, and rabbit kittens may be drowned in the nest if the weather is very bad or starve to death if their mother is killed. Rabbits are also prone to pest control measures, including diseases intro-

duced by man, namely Myxomatosis and Viral Haemorrhagic Disease (VHD). Males can expect a shorter life
than females because, as we will see later, they tend to be
away from the main group more often and thus more
exposed to predators. While rabbits can live for ten years
or more, in the wild a five-year-old is rare and it is unusual
for them to live for more than two years. Given the amount
of damage they can do, this may be of some consolation
to farmers.

Chasing
Rabbits chase other rabbits either because they do not
like them or because they like them very much. The first
case is related to territoriality and will be discussed in
more detail in the section on that subject. Here I will
consider the chasing that occurs between rabbits which
are positively interested in each other.

Such chasing makes up part of the courtship ritual of
rabbits and it is primarily the male who chases the female
of his choice. Rabbit courtship is not a long drawn out
affair and, as commercial rabbit breeders know, can be
extremely perfunctory, though this perhaps has more to
do with the confinement of the animals in a small space
than with the wishes of the rabbits in question.

Under more spacious, natural circumstances courtship
can involve several behaviours which may or may not result
in the male being allowed to mate with his chosen female.
A male rabbit, or buck, detects a female, or doe, that is
ready to be mated by his sense of smell. She emits substances known as pheromones which proclaim her sexual
state. Once the buck has identified the doe, he follows
her around, keeping five metres (16 feet) or more behind
her. Generally this is quite a slow progress around the
area, though of course it is the female who sets the pace.
Gradually, he moves closer in and starts to adopt a stiff-
legged strut and circle the female or parade in front of
her. She may take little notice of this show of maleness

and move away, thereby reinstating the original following behaviour, the courtship chase. Alternatively she may become quite flirtatious herself and do a little chasing of her own.

Digging

The 'diggers of underground passages' are very aptly named. Those of you who ride or walk across the countryside may well have experienced that sudden loss of balance as your or your horse's foot disappears down a rabbit hole. For Alice the experience was much more dramatic, since she disappeared entirely down a rabbit hole into Wonderland. Twisted ankles and broken legs are not unknown outcomes of the digging activity of rabbits.

Rabbits dig by scrabbling at the ground with their front paws to loosen the soil. They then use their powerful hind legs to kick the soil away. The main reason why rabbits dig is to create homes for themselves. Their warrens comprise an intricate network of tunnels, known as burrows. The size of the warren depends on the type of soil. Soft, unstable substances such as sand dunes will not support as extensive an underground complex as will the stronger soils of chalk downlands.

Many of the burrows are linked together in a maze of twisting underground rabbit routeways. These are very narrow, only about 15 cm (6 in) in diameter, so the rabbits can pass each other only at passing places where the burrow is widened out to about 40 cm (16 in). It is not known whether rabbits, like car drivers on country lanes, sometimes have disputes about who will reverse to allow the other to pass. The twisting nature and sharp turns of the burrow system help the rabbits confuse any weasel, stoat or Jack Russell Terrier small enough to enter, giving the rabbits the opportunity to escape through one of the many exits. A warren which covers 100 square metres (120 square yards) may have as many as 50 exits.

Rabbits are accomplished engineers. They construct

two forms of exit. The first, entrance/exit holes for normal use, are the ones you are most likely to be familiar with, particularly if your own rabbit has the opportunity to do a little bit of construction work in your garden. They are dug from above ground, tend to slope downwards quite gently and are characterised by mounds of earth nearby which may support a crop of ragwort, a plant which does well on disturbed earth which it needs to help its seeds germinate.

The second type is known as a bolt hole and is used in times of emergency, fleeing from a predator either above or below the ground. As bolt holes are dug from below ground there are no tell-tale mounds of earth nearby nor bare patches around the hole. In fact, they are often hidden in bushes. One can only surmise that the rabbits have a good mental map and can work out where to start digging to the surface in order to keep their bolt holes cunningly hidden. These holes are dug vertically from below, often from a depth of half a metre (18 in) or more. The advantage of a vertical drop is that while a rabbit can jump vertically up or easily drop down the burrow, this is not such an easy feat for a pursuing stoat or weasel.

Some burrows are blind alleys, going nowhere but ending in a widened 'room' called a side gallery. It is here that rabbits rest, groom and spend time reingesting their soft faecal pellets.

Some blind alleys, called nest stops, have exclusive access rights and are used by females as a site in which to build a nest and have their babies. They dig a new nest stop for each litter. Usually only the dominant females have their nest stops within the comparative safety of the warren system itself, though in areas prone to attack by weasels and stoats these females will often construct their nest stops away from the main warren. Females who rank lower in rabbit society usually dig nest stops some distance away. These external nest stops are quite shallow, descending sometimes as little as 15 cm (6 in) below ground and only extending for two metres (6½ ft). Nest stops have a single entrance/exit hole, perhaps to ensure that the babies do not get accidentally lost, a precaution helped by the downward slope tending to encourage very young rabbits to remain in the vicinity of the nest itself, or at least locate it without too much difficulty.

Rabbits also dig shallow, horseshoe-shaped depressions in the ground known as scrapes. Their purpose may be to expose some dry earth to roll in, to uncover some juicy young plant or, in winter, to expose anything edible. But the most common reason for these scrapes is to provide a site for rabbits, particularly males, to deposit small piles of faeces as a sign of occupation of the area. The earth revealed by the digging contrasts with the green sward surrounding it, acting rather like a billboard at the side of an open highway as seen in Spain or rural America.

Eating

All animals need to eat to live, but some humans, and some understimulated captive and domestic animals, seem to live to eat. Being overweight reduces the chances of being able to escape an enemy, or, if a predator, of being able to catch one's dinner. Obesity is a 'disease' of captivity. It is rare to see an overweight wild animal, even a rabbit living in an area with an abundance of food.

Animals are born in one of two states. First are species which produce 'precocial' offspring, that is young which are well developed and seem to be miniature adults. Examples include horses, sheep, cattle and cavies. The offspring of these species are able to eat grass right from the day they are born, although, as Paul McGreevy describes in *Why Does My Horse . . . ?*, they are better designed for suckling milk from their mothers. The second type of offspring is known as 'altricial'. These are born more or less undeveloped and helpless. In this category are species such as ourselves, whose young can hear and see from birth but are immobile. Other familiar species include the dog, cat, mouse and rabbit, whose young are born in an almost foetal state with their eyes and ears still not fully developed. These altricial species are totally dependent on milk for their early food.

Unlike other altricial species, baby rabbits in the nest spend very little time 'eating', only having access to their mother's nipples for a few minutes every day. This is not the state of affairs once they are weaned around 24 days after birth.

Young rabbits and adults spend a large proportion of their time awake eating. This is common for all grazing animals, though they may have different means of extracting the goodness from the grass. Some, such as horses, leave much of the work to the bacteria in their stomachs, continually topping up the supply for processing. Cows and sheep are ruminants which chew the cud—still time spent eating. It is important to remember that the rabbit evolved to be able to live in an area where available forage was sparse, low-quality scrub and herbage and they have developed the system of refection, which is described in more detail later. In these circumstances, an animal must spend a lot of time grazing in order to get sufficient nutrients and calories.

A rabbit is above the surface for about 12 hours in any 24-hour period. It spends most of that time eating (and looking out for predators while it chews the current mouthful). Three types of feeding behaviour have been described. 'Casual' feeding usually occurs near the burrow entrance and consists of idle nibbling, a little like me dipping into the biscuit barrel while writing this. In contrast there is 'voracious' feeding, where the rabbit grazes intently, following a straight feeding path, eating unselectively anything in its path—reminiscent of raiding the refrigerator. This voracious feeding activity is often seen in more inclement weather when the rabbit is perhaps wishing to fill its belly as quickly as possible so that it can retreat to its burrow out of the wind and rain. Finally, there is what is known as the 'normal' feeding pattern, where the rabbit moves slowly in a zigzag pattern selecting tasty plant species and tender young leaves to nibble.

Fouling

The primary function of fouling, or defecation, is to rid the body of waste products. But where and how faeces are deposited can also be used as a form of communication.

Most rabbit faeces are randomly deposited as the animal moves around, feeding or socialising with other colony members. Rabbit faeces are rich in nitrogen and this random deposition means that rabbits act as their own agriculturists, fertilising the ground as they go, and thereby helping to ensure that more grass will grow to be eaten another day. Adding rabbit droppings to your compost heap is a very good idea.

Rabbits also deposit their droppings in scrapes marking the warren's territorial boundaries. But the most impressive use of droppings has to be the creation of latrines. These are communal toilets used by all members of the colony and comprise thousands of tightly packed, dry faecal pellets. Often the latrines are located on a slight rise in the terrain, making them even more obvious to any other rabbit. These latrine sites provide visual and olfactory signals to both members and non-members of the colony. They probably have two major functions related to marking the boundary of the group's territory. The first is to signal to the residents that it is their territory, thus enhancing their confidence that they are 'at home'. This is comparable to us humans feeling more relaxed when we see familiar landmarks or our front gate which inform us we are on our own property. The second function is the same as that performed by our own fences and gates, namely to warn outsiders that this is our territory. Latrine sites warn any rabbit from another colony that it is entering the territory of a different colony and should be alert to the fact that it may be chased away or attacked by the residents.

Grooming

A rabbit doing its 'toilette' is really cute to watch. Rabbits lick their forepaws and then wipe them over their face and ears, often pulling the latter down over their eyes to get the backs of the ears really clean. They also spend time nibbling their legs, back, haunches and belly with rapid, precise movements of their teeth in order to dislodge and remove any prickles, dirt and loose fur. Scratching the fur with the hind feet is also part of grooming, a behaviour which takes some practice as anyone who has watched a baby rabbit enthusiastically scratching the air instead of its head will agree.

Grooming is an extremely important behaviour, since a well-kept coat will provide better insulation against the weather and reduce the chances of the rabbit falling ill due to infestations of fleas, mites and lice. Rabbits are fastidiously clean creatures, spending some 16 per cent of their daily activity in grooming. Wild rabbits are covered in a short dense coat of fur. The soft undercoat, so loved by fashionable ladies and felt manufacturers in the past, is overlaid with curly fine hairs and guard hairs. Once a year the rabbit sheds and replaces its entire coat. The moult starts in March and is completed, resulting in a thick winter coat, by October. It is particularly important to keep the area around the anus clean and free of tangled fur. Matted fur here may mean the rabbits cannot pass the soft, moist faeces it produces for reingestion. A rabbit that is unable to do so is likely to lose condition rapidly as it cannot obtain all the nutrients it requires to live.

Rabbits also indulge in mutual grooming, known as allogrooming. It is not unusual to see rabbits lying close together, licking and nibbling each others' ears and heads. We know from work done on wild horses that such behaviour can slow the heart rate of the participants, suggesting that it is a pleasant, relaxing behaviour. We also know that being massaged by another human is equally relaxing for ourselves. Research has shown that simply stroking (allogrooming) our companion animals can reduce our blood pressure and even help us recover from heart attacks. It may well be that the grooming of one rabbit by another helps them both relax and strengthens any relationship between them. Of course it is also easier for someone else to get to those tricky bits like the back of the head or neck.

Home ranges

An animal's home range is the area it uses frequently, often where it forages and socialises. Unlike the group's territory, the home range is not defended and may well overlap with the home ranges of other colony groups. If you like, my territory is my home and garden, but my home range includes my local shops, office and pub.

The size of the home range of a rabbit group depends primarily on the amount of food available. If food is plentiful and on the doorstep, so to speak, then there is little point in travelling far in order to feed and running a greater risk of being caught by a predator. In some places, such as the sand-dune complex of the Isle of Lindisfarne off the north-east coast of England, rabbits have to travel several hundred metres (yards) from their burrows in the sand dunes to the slacks near the shore where they can feed. Home-range size may also fluctuate slightly during the year as food becomes more or less scarce around the warren site. This may apply particularly to rabbits which make their living off crops and have to travel further afield when the crop is harvested.

Infanticide

The trait of infanticide shows a darker side of the rabbit's character. Under natural conditions this seems to be a behaviour of females. Infanticide occurs for three reasons.

The first might be considered accidental infanticide. This is when a female rabbit gets somewhat overenthusiastic when cleaning her newborn young, during which she ingests the umbilical cord and placenta. This may result in a baby losing just an ear tip or it may mean the baby dies as the mother unwittingly eats a vital bit of gut along with the umbilical cord. This is thought to be fairly rare among wild rabbits, though it is quite common in inexperienced domestic animals.

Infanticide is also common among rabbits living in high-density populations. In such stressful circumstances, or where the nest is disturbed, the female may well resort to killing and eating her young, apparently on purpose. While we might find this distressing we should remember that from the rabbit's point of view it is more efficient to reuse all that protein oneself than leave it for a predator to benefit from.

The third source of infanticide is from females other than the kittens' own mother. Female rabbits are not very tolerant of the young of other females, even those of the same colony who are likely to be their close relatives. A doe coming across a nest of kittens which are not her own will have no hesitation in killing the occupants. This again may seem rather brutal, but in the scheme of things it makes some sense. Reducing the population of other youngsters means that her own young will have less competition in the survival game and be more likely to grow up and reproduce successfully. Even after they are weaned and taking part in colony life, young rabbits are not immune from being killed by females other than their mother.

Jumping

Jumping is not behaviour one perhaps easily associates with rabbits. They tend to go under rather than over wherever possible and they do not meet many obstacles which require them to indulge in feats of propulsion through the air. But this does not mean they cannot jump. Certainly young rabbits will take to hopping fast and leaping into the air, twisting their backs before they land and so changing direction. This apparently playful behaviour allows them to practise and fine tune the muscle coordination needed for this feat, which may prove to be a lifesaver. When pursued by a predator, rabbits will bolt for the nearest hole, frequently changing direction en route in order to evade capture.

Kittens

There are few sights more endearing than that of a young rabbit kitten, newly emerged from the nest. Its tiny, fluffy, rounded body and head, topped with neatly formed ears and wide curious eyes surely justify their immortalisation in children's literature with names reflecting their 'cuddle' factor such as Flopsy, Cottontail and Benjamin Bunny.

Far from being cute, newborn rabbits are really quite ugly. They have pink, naked, elongated bodies with tiny, almost useless legs and huge heads. The eyes are undeveloped and do not open until some ten days after birth. The ears are small and lie flat against the head, only becoming functional after seven days. On the other hand, baby rabbits are sensitive to touch and temperature and their noses are very efficient right from birth.

As we will see in more detail in the section on parenting, rabbit mothers spend very little time with their babies and hardly interact with them, unlike other species with altricial or undeveloped young. This means that nestling rabbit kittens need ways to keep themselves warm, clean and safe and ensure they are in the right place when their mother comes to feed them. The physiology and behaviour of rabbit kittens has evolved in a sophisticated manner to cope with this overall lack of tender loving care.

Kittens can distinguish between the scent of their mother and that of other rabbits or other species. They recognise their mother from scent that she deposits with some faeces at the entrance to the nest stop. This scent, called anal gland secretion, is also deposited in the nest itself as the doe leaves a few faecal pellets in the bedding. The kittens are attracted to their mother's scent and are thus deterred from wandering too far up the nest burrow and potentially into danger from another doe or a predator. The kittens also use their noses to locate a nipple during nursing. Having first located the mother's fur as she stands over them to nurse, the babies follow a scent gradient from her belly to her nipples. This implies that this particular scent, which only seems to be effective over a very short range, gets stronger nearer to a nipple. Either the high concentration of the odour at the nipple, or perhaps a second odour, causes the kitten to stop its searching behaviour, grasp the nipple and start sucking. These tiny, blind, deaf creatures may take 12 seconds to find a nipple during the first couple of days, and suckling is frequently interrupted as the kitten loses hold. By the fifth day of life, however, the kitten, still blind and deaf, is an expert, able to find a nipple and start suckling within three seconds!

The behaviour of kittens for the first couple of weeks is quite regulated and is centred on the time of nursing. After this period the kittens are more mobile and exploratory and will begin to spend time away from the nest. At this later age they will emerge on to the surface and investigate the world in the immediate vicinity of the nest burrow entrance. But they do not stray too far from the scent of their mother's faeces which enables them to return to the nest in time for their daily meal of mother's milk.

Immediately after birth, rabbit kittens are very active and vocal and their mother allows them to suckle briefly before she leaves them alone. Following her departure the rabbits quickly burrow under the nest material. After this their behaviour follows a regular pattern, based on a 22-hour cycle. Rabbit kittens are fed by their mother approximately once every 24 hours, so the 22-hour activity cycle of kittens ensures they are ready for their mother's visit even if she decides to come an hour or so early.

Within 15 minutes after nursing all the kittens have burrowed down into the nest. There they stay tightly grouped together in its warm centre. This huddle of kittens means that the warmth of all the bodies keeps each individual warm and cosy. Newborn rabbits are unable to keep themselves warm but are able to detect temperature differences of only 0.2 °C (0.4 °F). This has two effects. First, kittens will seek out their brothers and sisters to snuggle up to and they will move away from the cold bodies of any of their littermates which have died. Secondly, there is a continual, slow, circular movement of the group in the nest as those on the top of the heap get slightly cool and burrow down through their siblings to get to the warmer spots below.

After some 22 hours the whole group becomes more active, slowly pushing their way up to the surface of the nest. Here they gently mill around each other, frequently lifting their disproportionately large heads to sniff the air. They use their sense of smell to detect their mother's arrival, which is greeted with an outburst of activity. The kittens shove and push to reach a nipple, rapidly moving their heads as they follow the scent gradient which helps them locate and attach to the desired source of food. Once attached, the kittens brace their tiny back legs to help support their elongated bodies. With their front feet they start to paddle their mother's belly, stimulating her to let down her milk. This ejection of milk only happens at the end of the nursing episode, when the mother has been sufficiently stimulated by several pairs of little legs pummelling her body. But her babies are not patient enough to stay on the first nipple they find until the squirt of milk arrives. Instead each kitten changes position four or five times, about once very 30 seconds, pushing the others out of the way as it attaches to a different nipple. Perhaps this serves to ensure that the doe is stimulated all the way down the line of nipples and does indeed let down her milk.

Having squirted out her milk, the mother rabbit abruptly leaves the nest and returns up the burrow to the exit. Occasionally a kitten, perhaps hoping for more, will not have let go of the nipple and is dragged part way up the burrow. The slope down to the nest of the burrow floor and the olfactory cues of the nest itself soon help the kitten find its way back to its brothers and sisters.

Immediately after nursing, all the kittens urinate at the surface of the nest, before burrowing back down to its warm, dry centre. This ability of rabbit babies to be able to urinate by themselves is not common amongst altricial species and has evolved as an anti-predator strategy, related to the minimal care shown by the mother. Other species such as cats, rats and dogs all lick the young in the appropriate area to stimulate them to urinate and defecate. The fact that rabbits can manage this all by themselves is worth remembering should you ever hand rear a rabbit kitten. Once it has been fed, either put it down or hold it facing away from you, or be prepared to get wet. Urinating immediately after nursing means that a kitten does not have to leave the warmth of the nest in order to relieve itself, and performing at the surface of the nest ensures that the bedding into which they snuggle down does not get damp. All rather clever, really.

During the first 11 days the kittens spend less and less time covered by the nest material. This is in part due to their increasing size and also to the growth of fur during this period, making them less dependent on the nest material for warmth. At about eight days old, they start to nibble the nest material and by 12 days have munched their way through most of it. They also begin to eat the faecal pellets left in the nest by their mother. This may be how they obtain the bacteria, known as gut flora, which they will need to digest the plant food they will eat when weaned. The flavour of the pellets and the milk they receive from their mother also provides the babies with information about the sort of plants they should eat later in life.

By 18 days of age the kittens are exploring the world outside, rushing back to the safety of the nest burrow should they be frightened by anything. At around 24 days they are abandoned by their mother, who simply does not return to nurse them, leaving them to fend for themselves and to start to become active members of warren life. It will take another three months for them to reach sexual maturity and eight before they are fully grown at nine months of age. By that time they will have changed from naked, ugly creatures weighing some 50 g (2 oz) at birth to fleet-footed, big-eared rabbits weighing 1.5 kg (3¼ lb) perhaps with young of their own.

Language
As we have seen, rabbits spend most of their life in darkness and consequently tend not to use visual signals as a main channel for communicating with each other. The primary means by which rabbits inform each other about their whereabouts, sexual status and health is olfaction. You may think that vocalisations would also be a useful means of communication in the semi or complete darkness of the rabbit world. In fact, rabbits are almost silent, a precaution against attracting the attention of predators. Communicating by sound would give a predator the opportunity of locating an individual rabbit's whereabouts to the benefit of the predator and the detriment of the rabbit.

The rabbit's vocal repertoire is thus very limited when we compare it to other species with whom we spend our lives, such as cats or dogs. Vocalisations tend to denote pleasure, pain or aggression which may be rooted in anger or fear.

Like cats, rabbits make a purring sound when they are contented. They also produce a soft clicking noise which you may have noticed when your rabbit has eaten a particularly tasty morsel. A quiet grinding of the teeth also seems to mean that a rabbit is relaxed and contented.

A rabbit who does not wish to be approached makes its position quite clear by loudly grinding its teeth or emitting a series of grunts and growls. If that does not do the trick in deterring the oncomer, then the rabbit will hiss. Loud teeth-grinding can also be a sign of pain. But the most haunting and eerie noise a rabbit produces is a scream, which sounds remarkably like a human baby in intense pain. Rabbits only scream when they are extremely frightened as when they are being attacked by a predator, in extremis. It no doubt serves as a desperate attempt to scare off the predator and as a warning to any other rabbits in the vicinity.

Baby rabbits which are still in the nest also use noise to try and scare off predators. If disturbed, a litter of youngsters, even though they may still be blind and deaf, will vocalise loudly and 'jump' up in a synchronised startle response. While this is unlikely to deter a larger or more experienced predator, it might be sufficient to ward off an attack by a small or young animal such as a fox cub.

Mating
Courtship in rabbits is designed to bring both the male and female rabbit to a state of sexual excitement to enable a successful mating. A fertile mating results in a gestation period lasting approximately 30 days. An infertile mating may cause the female to become pseudo-pregnant, a state usually lasting for about 16 days during which she is unable to conceive.

Unlike human females, the oestrous cycle in the rabbit does not end with ovulation, that is the release of eggs from the oestrus into the Fallopian tubes. Instead, rabbits have a system known as 'spontaneous ovulation'. This means that eggs are produced in the ovaries but are not released into the Fallopian tubes until the female is mated. This again shows how the pressures of the rabbit's original harsh environment have affected its physiology and behaviour. Should copulation not occur, then 'unused' eggs are reabsorbed into the body, rather than being wastefully eliminated. With copulation acting as the trigger for the release of eggs, there is a much greater chance of any individual egg being fertilised, as it is only released when sperms are present.

During the breeding season, does have an oestrous cycle of approximately seven days. It takes three to four days for an egg to mature in the ovary and thus to be ready for release into the Fallopian tubes. Once the egg is ready, for the next two or three days the doe is receptive to a male, that is, she is willing to mate, which may result in the successful fertilisation of the eggs. Should copulation not occur, the mature eggs are reabsorbed and some new ones begin to mature. If the environmental conditions are good, with warm weather and plenty of food, the female will spend the whole season in almost continuous oestrus. Even when she is pregnant the behavioural cycle continues and pregnant females are often remated around the fourteenth day of gestation. Indeed, females are generally fairly receptive to males, though the frequency of mating does decline during pregnancy.

Rabbits can, in fact, conceive throughout the year, but this is rare in the wild. There is a sharply defined onset to the breeding season with almost all females becoming pregnant within seven days of each other. Matings which occur before the breeding season tend not to result in ovulation. This suggests that the onset of the breeding season is determined by a change in the reproductive physiology of the females, probably in response to the change in the day length of early spring. With the shortening of the days in late summer the fecundity of both males and females declines. Both sperm production and testicle weight of the males decrease and the testicles regress into the abdominal cavity, only descending again the following year.

Nest building

The expectant mother starts preparing for the birth of her kittens during the last two weeks of her pregnancy. The first chore is to find a suitable spot to dig out a nest burrow which will not be too exposed to either predators or weather. Heavy rainfall can result in the nest burrow being flooded and nestling rabbits are extremely vulnerable to drowning. You may have noticed short abandoned burrows in fields. These are 'test' sites which have turned out to be unsuitable. Old burrows from a previous season may be used, but a doe rarely uses the same burrow more than once in a season, creating a new one for each litter of kittens. Once an appropriate site is found the doe digs out the burrow.

Some time in the last week of her pregnancy, perhaps even as late as the day she is due to give birth, the doe starts to prepare the nest itself. She gathers grasses and dead plants which she carries in her mouth down to the bottom of the burrow. It takes many journeys to collect enough bedding to construct the nest. Once sufficient has been amassed, the doe hollows out the centre of the mound with her head and front paws. She then lines the interior hollow completely with soft fur which she pulls out with her teeth from her belly, flanks and chest. The final construction is like a round vase. There is a narrow neck at the top, swelling out into a warm, dry, comfortable, fur-lined chamber into which she gently places her new-born young.

Order

The life of the wild rabbit is one of order in terms of both time and social structure. Of course this statement could be applied generally, as all animals follow some more or less rigid pattern of daily activity, yearly seasons and interactions with other members of the species.

In terms of daily activity, the rabbit is naturally a creature of habit, emerging from its burrow at dusk and returning soon after dawn. As we have also seen, its breeding behaviour is regulated by the earth's orbit around the sun changing the ratio of day to night through the seasons. This annual order of the seasons also influences the social order of the warren inhabitants.

A large warren may provide living space for 50 or more rabbits. The warren can be thought of as a village, whose total population is known as a colony. The colony comprises several smaller, distinct social groups. An individual group may consist of only two animals, usually a male and female. Groups rarely contain more than eight animals, and females usually outnumber males. The females in a group tend to be closely related. Each group has a social order designed to maintain harmony amongst its members.

Among the males this hierarchy is quite rigid, with the dominant male, often larger and older than the other males, getting priority access to females for mating and the best feeding and resting sites. These so-called dominance hierarchies are not maintained by the 'top' rabbit being aggressive or bullying. Rather, as with dogs and horses, the other rabbits weigh up their chances of winning a possible fight and, if the odds seem stacked against them, they show submissive behaviour and give way to the more dominant animal. As the young males mature they are likely to challenge the dominant buck and are usually driven away from the group before they reach full maturity. These young bucks disperse to join new groups within the colony, or even leave the warren altogether and try their luck in a new one. Young males do tend to be accepted into new warrens once the breeding season is over for that year. In this way the rabbit colonies avoid becoming inbred. Between being sent packing by their natal group and finding a new home, these young males tend to live on the surface, resting in shallow hollows or scrapes hidden under bushes. During this period of roaming and surface living they are known as 'satellites'. Other satellite males are often old animals which have lost their position of authority in the group and have been driven out by a younger, stronger male.

Amongst the females there is also an order of seniority, often with a single dominant doe. But this hierarchy is much more relaxed than that between males, and the does are more tolerant of the other females in their group, at least for most of the year. During the breeding season, female rabbits can become exceptionally aggressive to those females they had spent the autumn and winter lying next to, nibbling each others' ears and being generally friendly. While males compete for access to females for mating, access to males is not a problem for females and the majority will spend the breeding season pregnant. What is imperative for does is that they find safe, dry places in which to build their nests. These may not be all that plentiful, and females have been known to fight to the death over which of them will be able to claim ownership rights of a particular breeding site.

Parenting
Mammal species adopt one of four types of parenting. Those with precocial, well-developed young, such as horses and sheep, show the 'following system'. Within a few hours of birth the young are able to follow the mother around her home range and stay close to her for protection, warmth and nourishment. Other species with precocial young, such as the rabbit's close relative the hare, have evolved a system known as 'lying-out'. In this case

the young lie quietly hidden in the long grass or bracken, returning to the place of their birth once a day to meet up with their mother to be fed.

The vast majority of species with altricial young usually adopt the 'shelter system' of care. In this system the mothers, and in some cases the fathers too, act as the main life-support system. They make a nest and spend most of their time curled up with their helpless offspring. A mother rat, for instance, will spend over 90 per cent of her day with her newborn babies. The parents clean, feed, protect and keep the babies warm until they are old enough to do so for themselves.

A few, very few species with altricial young show what is called 'absentee' parenting. This is characterised by the young being left in a nest separate from the one used by the parents. They are not being warmed or directly protected by a parent, and long intervals pass between nursing bouts. There is also a lack, or virtual lack, of parental behaviours such as carrying or cleaning the young. Of all the animals studied to date, only the tree shrew, *Tupaia belengari* (a primitive primate), the pika, *Ochotona princeps* (a distant cousin of the rabbit), the members of the genus *Sylvilagus* (the cottontail rabbits of North America) and the European rabbit (the subject of this book) show this form of care. And of this select band of species, only the European rabbit has truly altricial young. While the young of tree shrews, pikas and *Sylvilagus* are also born blind they are able to thermoregulate, that is maintain their body temperature, at least for a short while, away from the nest. These, then, are known as semi-altricial young. Human young are also considered semi-altricial, being able to thermoregulate, see and hear, but humans, like dogs, cats and rats, show the shelter system of care.

So it can be said that the European rabbit, ancestor of all our domestic rabbits, it almost unique in terms of the way it rears its young. I am going to describe this system

and then speculate about how it may have come about that
the rabbit is so peculiar in this aspect of its life strategy.

Studies of the parenting behaviour of wild rabbits have
concentrated on the nursing behaviour of females who
have had their young in nest burrows located away from
the main warren. These studies have tended to report that
female rabbits visit the nest once in a 24-hour period to
nurse their young. These visits last about three minutes,
and consist only of nursing bouts. However, my own work
on the parental behaviour of the domestic rabbit suggests
that the picture may not be quite so simple. Of course, it
could be that the maternal behaviour of the rabbits I
studied has been altered by domestication, although this
is unlikely in that the differences were only slight, and
would be unlikely to have occurred through domestication. The rationale for this statement is that humans
can only modify animals through artificial selection, that
in this they can only work with the genetic material available. Though mutations can and do occur, they tend to
be fairly limited in effect. My studies suggested that rabbits
show some degree of parental behaviour similar to that
seen in species which adopt the shelter system. Why this
may be is a subject to which I will return shortly. An
alternative, and more likely, explanation of why this had
not been previously recorded is that a female which gives
birth in the safety of the warren may act differently from
one whose young are born in the more vulnerable external nest stops.

In my own studies of rabbits during pregnancy and
lactation, I recorded the behaviour of females living either
on their own or with their mate in large indoor enclosures.
The paired females were in a situation similar to that of
a dominant doe which would give birth to her young
within the warren complex, that is the nest burrow would
be located near to other colony members. In many cases,
as on Lindisfarne, the only other colony member may
indeed be her mate. The description of parenting

behaviour given here is a summary of my own work and that of other researchers conducted over the last 40 years.

When a rabbit kitten is born, its mother licks it clean and eats the umbilical cord and placenta. She then gives her young their first feed. The first few nursing bouts may be as long as five minutes. This is probably because the kittens are rather inefficient both in attaching to a nipple and in stimulating their mother to let down her milk. As they become more efficient, the nursing bouts shorten to between two and three minutes' duration. On average females nurse their young 1.3 times a day, though one female I recorded nursed her babies seven times in a single day. The normal interval between nursing sessions is from 23 to 25 hours, which means the kittens' daily cycle of moving to the surface of the nest every 22 hours ensures they are prepared for their mother's arrival. Sometimes, though, they have a long wait as intervals of 27 hours between nursing bouts are not uncommon; in some cases the females in my study did not visit their young to feed them for 36 hours or more—with no harm to their young. Nursing tends to occur between 8 p.m. and 6 a.m., that is during the normal activity period of the adults.

At the end of a nursing bout the female drops her head and arches her back, presumably to dislodge the young from her nipples. She then leaves the burrow, carefully plugging the entrance with earth to stop any unwelcome visitors. Around 18 days after birth, she stops plugging the burrow entrance so securely, thus allowing the kittens to start to emerge and explore the world outside. After 25 days she ceases to return and her young are now on their own.

According to most books on rabbits that is the extent of the females' maternal behaviour, and the males are traditionally believed to be indifferent or even aggressive to nestling kittens. This would appear to be something of a myth, though it is fair to say that rabbits are not the most solicitous of parents. They do show some parental behaviours beyond those already described.

Both male and female rabbits spend some proportion of their time in the nest with the young. Compared to other species with altricial young, such as the mouse and gerbil, where both parents are involved in the process of rearing their brood, this time is minimal. For example, while mouse and gerbil fathers spend between 50 and 80 per cent of their time in the nest, the figure for rabbit fathers is only 1 per cent. Excluding the time spent nursing, rabbit mothers also spend only about 1 per cent of their day with their young. This time is spend rearranging or adding to the nest material (including, in the case of females, pulling out more fur), being vigilant and scent-marking the area. Does have been recorded licking their young and my own observations showed that males too will sniff and lick their nestling young, and both sexes cover them with nest material.

Being vigilant and scent-marking the area around the young can be classed as protective behaviour. This might not be expected from an animal whose main form of defence is to run away and which does not, apparently, actively defend its young. It may just be that the location of the nest and brief time spent in its vicinity means that active defence is not required frequently and thus has not been seen. Certainly domestic does can be quite aggressive if you attempt to interfere with their nest.

The albeit limited amount of care given directly to the young in terms of licking them and covering them with the nest material has been the subject of some speculation about the origins of the absentee form of parental care. Briefly, one argument suggests that absenteeism is an evolutionary early form of care; the other suggests that the rabbit's ancestors originally showed the shelter system of care but have modified it dramatically in response to the large risk to the young from predators and from other females. This is a rather obtuse, academic question. Whilst

I personally find it interesting (it was, after all, an aspect of my thesis), it can only be speculative until some scientist makes Dr Who's time machine, the Tardis, a reality and we can go back and study the behaviour of the rabbit's ancestors.

Quantity

While, for some, rabbits are delightful creatures which enhance our walks in the countryside, for others they are no more than a pest which requires severe control measures. Rabbits cause immense damage to crops. At the height of the rabbit population explosion in Britain, around the time of the Second World War, damage was estimated to be worth some £300 million (about $500 million) per annum. There were literally millions of rabbits, with about 40 million being caught every year for their fur and meat. In 1953 Myxomatosis was introduced to Britain to control the rabbit. It was certainly very effec-

The situation was desperate

tive to begin with, killing over 99 per cent of the rabbit population. But the few surviving rabbits were resistant and soon the population increased. By the mid-1980s the rabbit numbers in crop-growing areas, such as the southeast of England, were back to pre-Myxomatosis levels.

The best documented data on the growth of a rabbit population comes from Australia. All of the millions of wild rabbits in Australia were descended from 24 animals introduced by one Thomas Austen in 1859. He brought these animals from England to his estate in Victoria to remind him of home and provide him with some sport. Only six years later over 20,000 rabbits had been killed on his estate alone. Seven years after their introduction the rabbits had so increased in number that they had spread across country and were found over 800 km (500 miles) away in Queensland. The situation was desperate. The Australians tried to stop the rabbits by shooting them, gassing them and ripping up their burrows. Myxomatosis was introduced in the 1950s, but its initial success did not last and, as with Britain, Australia once again had a major pest problem.

In the late 1990s a new disease was discovered, Viral Haemorrhagic Disease (VHD). This has been introduced as the latest weapon in man's war against the rabbit. It has proved to be as effective as Myxomatosis and has killed off most of the wild population in Australia. However, total eradication of the rabbit requires that those animals remaining need to be exterminated by more traditional means. VHD is a nasty disease with the rabbit suffering internal bleeding in the gut, lungs and urinary tract. Death is usually quite quick. As far is known, this disease is specific to rabbits. Viruses are, however, extremely adept at being able to alter and become a disease for other species. It is to be hoped that this particular form of biological control remains specific to rabbits and does not harm other animal species, be they native fauna of Australia or any other part of the world.

Refection

Refection is a process of digestion which the rabbit has evolved to help it extract the maximum amount of goodness from every mouthful it eats. The vegetation is sliced into small pieces and ground into a fine pulp by the forward and sideways motion of the teeth. This pulp is then swallowed and passed into the stomach, where it is further broken down before progressing through the small intestine to the caecum and appendix. Unlike the human appendix which is no longer functional, the rabbit's appendix and caecum are very important features of its digestive system. Here resides a large population of benevolent bacteria, whose job in life is to break down the tough cellulose walls of the plant cells and so release the nutrients which are absorbed by the rabbit's gut and turned into muscle, bones, fur—turned into rabbit.

Now comes what may appear, at first glance, to be something of a design fault. It would seem logical for the nutrients to be absorbed in the part of the gut reached after the appendix and caecum bacteria factory, but in fact absorption takes place in the small intestine passed through earlier, just after the stomach. Nature has resolved this problem by refection, literally the partaking of a meal, in this case for the second time.

. . . the rabbit swiftly bows its head between its back legs
and catches the pellet . . .

The now unrecognisable mush of what was once grass passes down through to the rectum where it is pressed into small round balls and covered in mucus. These soft, damp pellets are then ejected one at a time from the anus. As the pellet passes into the open, the rabbit swiftly bows its head between its back legs and catches the pellet in its mouth before it hits the ground. The pellet is then ground up again, swallowed and passed through the stomach. This time, all the nutrients, now released, are taken up in the small intestine and passed into the bloodstream to be utilised throughout the rabbit's body. What remains continues through the system and is ejected as hard, tightly packed droppings left on the surface of the ground.

Rabbits tend to produce soft droppings for reprocessing during the day and the hard pellets at night when they are above ground. This means they can do much of their digestion underground, only leaving the safety of the burrow in order to fill their stomachs. On cold, wet nights this can be a very short time indeed.

Scent-marking

As was described earlier, rabbits use their faeces as a means of communicating with other members of their group and outsiders. They do this by coating the droppings with a secretion from their anal glands.

Rabbits also have glands under their chin which exude a clear substance easily smelt by other rabbits, but not detectable by us humans who really do have a poor sense of smell compared to most other animals. Rabbits of both sexes have these chin glands and will mark prominent objects in their environment, including each other. They rub their chin gently on the object, leaving tiny amounts of secretion. Male rabbits are particularly enthusiastic chin-rubbers and the fur on their chin will often become matted with dirt and secretion as they mark out their territory.

Territorial behaviour

Rabbits maintain small territories within their home range. These are actively marked with pheromones from their anal and chin glands.

The maintenance and defence of territorial boundaries is the major occupation of males during the breeding season—apart from eating and mating. While all males in a group will be involved, it is the dominant male who is primarily responsible for seeing off any intruder. Indeed, often such intruders will be dominant males from other groups out to see if they can extend their property rights.

Obviously, a male on such a sortie will try to avoid any of the resident males. When two males do meet, one of three things can happen. First, the intruder may decide that discretion is the better part of valour and retreat across the (to us invisible) boundary, often chased to the frontier by the resident male. Alternatively, he may attempt to defuse the situation by adopting a submissive posture. This involves lying close to the ground and flattening his ears close to his head. The resident male will make his position and feelings known by slowly approaching the intruder, nibbling the grass in short bursts interspersed with chinning the ground or digging it frantically with his forepaws. If this does the trick, the intruder will beat a hasty retreat, followed by the triumphant resident male.

Thirdly, if the intruder has decided that he has a chance of deposing the resident male, he will neither retreat nor adopt a submissive posture but stand his ground. In this case the situation will hot up and a lot of posturing will occur before any real damage is done. Both males show off their prowess by scraping the ground, running past each other with a stiff-legged gait and chasing each other. Should there still be doubt about who is the stronger then the males will start to fight and the fur will fly.

Territorial defence is rather more relaxed during the

non-breeding season when new animals can join groups or start new ones of their own.

Urine

Rabbits, like cats, can pass urine in two distinct ways. The first and most common method is simply squatting slightly and emptying their bladder. The second is called 'spraying'. Spraying is usually performed by male rabbits either at a subordinate male or as an act of courtship towards a female. In the latter case it has a special name, 'enurination'.

The act of spraying is very quick and requires the male to run past the other rabbit, lifting up his hindquarters as he goes and twisting them as he emits a jet of urine. They rarely miss their target.

Visual communication

Visual signals do not comprise a large part of the rabbit's communication system. Given that they spend so much of their time in the dark this is perhaps not surprising. There are, however, variations in body posture and placement of the ears denoting submission, fear, aggressive intent, contentment and being relaxed.

A relaxed rabbit will lie either on its side or on its abdomen with its hind limbs stretched out behind. Alternatively the rabbit may squat down with its legs tucked beneath and ears folded against the head.

A submissive rabbit will crouch down, making itself appear small and non-threatening. Indeed, submission is generally indicated in the animal world by making the body appear smaller, often avoiding eye contact with the more dominant animal. This is very clearly seen in dogs which tuck their body up, lower it and their head and look away from the more dominant dog or person.

The posture taken by a fearful rabbit is very similar to that of a submissive animal. The main difference is that when it is frightened, the rabbit's facial muscles will become taut, giving the impression that the eyes are about to pop out of its head. The body will be pressed into the ground and ears flattened tightly against the head. This is an attempt by the rabbit to appear as inconspicuous as possible while keeping a watchful eye and nose on the whereabouts of the cause of its fear.

Rabbits shake their heads to denote irritation or dislike, of a strange smell or taste, for example. This is sometimes followed by a further bit of visual communication, perhaps the one with which we are most familiar, namely the dramatic thumping of the back legs on the ground, both a visual and auditory signal of potential danger. A rabbit who is really concerned about such a possibility will then retreat, at speed, to its burrow, raising its hindquarters as it runs and thus displaying the white underside, or scut, of its tail. This white patch of fur stands out against the darker body and is visible to other rabbits, even in low light levels, and serves as a strong signal for all of them to seek the shelter and safety of the burrow.

Weapons
Rabbits can certainly pull a hefty punch, though they tend to use their well-muscled hind legs rather than their shorter, weaker front paws. Rabbits will box with their front legs, raising themselves upright or lunging forward to back up their position with a sharp bite. When you consider those teeth are designed for slicing through tough stems and even tree bark, or crunching carrots, it is easy to imagine the pain of a rabbit bite . . . assuming you have not been unlucky enough to have felt the real thing.

Rabbits are not overly aggressive creatures but when they do fight they do so with fervour and with no regard to the Queensberry rules. They fight by grabbing hold of the opponent with teeth and front paws, while delivering a series of solid punches with the hind feet. The effect of these punches is enhanced by the strong, sharp nails which can rip open the belly of another rabbit. Fighting is not restricted to competition between males; does, too, sometimes fight to the death for nest sites and will also attack recently emerged kittens which are not their own. All rabbits are also more than capable of putting up a brave and sometimes successful fight for their life if caught by a predator.

X-breeds

I am sometimes asked if rabbits and hares can breed together. The answer is simply, no. Though there is a domestic breed of rabbit called the Belgian Hare, this is misleading. It is in fact all rabbit, and its rangy hare-like appearance is down to artificial selection by breeders to produce a long-legged beast.

There are several species of rabbit around the world, some of which, such as the North American cottontails, are also reminiscent of hares. However, these are distant cousins both of our European rabbit and of hares, different species which cannot successfully interbreed with either hares, domestic rabbits or their forebear the European rabbit.

Yarns

Rabbits and their cousins hares have often been incorporated into myths and superstition. In some cases there has been a lot of confusion between the species, and sometimes whether it is a rabbit or a hare seems to make little difference to the outcome.

One well-known superstition concerns the carrying of a hare's or rabbit's foot as a lucky talisman to ward off ill-health and bad luck. Of course to be effective it had to be prepared in just the right way. Without the joint a rabbit's or hare's foot was completely useless. In the mid-seventeenth century carrying such an item was believed to be a sure cure for stomach ache, and Samuel Pepys certainly thought so. It is likely that this belief originated with the Africans brought to Britain and the Americas as slaves. In Africa hares (and so their look-alikes, rabbits) had long been seen as mystical creatures, a tradition descended from the ancient animist religions. The rubbing of a hare's or rabbit's foot was certain to bring you good luck, but only if it was the animal's left foot.

People can never agree on anything, it seems. Even in different parts of England superstitions vary. In Somerset rabbits are associated with witchcraft and are thus not to be tampered with. One suspects that carrying a rabbit's foot in that part of the world would not be popular. Somerset residents were not alone in their avoidance of rabbit parts. Many fishing folk believed (and some still do) that taking any part of a rabbit on board a boat or ship would be a sure recipe for disaster. Being caught with a rabbit's foot in your pocket could mean you had quite a swim home as your shipmates threw you and the offending item overboard.

One area where there seems to be no disagreement is the rabbit's notoriety for its ability to reproduce. It has long been a symbol of sin and lust and was often portrayed as a companion of Venus, the Goddess of Love. This association of rabbits and fecundity has been passed down to this day in the form of the Easter Bunny. The pre-Christian tradition had a festival every spring to the Goddess Eastre, who was attended by a hare (later deposed and replaced by a rabbit), to herald the beginning of spring and the associated birth of livestock and growth of crops. This festival was incorporated into the new Christian festival, Easter. The traditional Easter eggs represent the forces of creation and recreation, another aspect of the wonders of spring.

Zoonoses

Zoonoses are those diseases which can be transferred from one species to another, in particular from animals to humans. This is not usually a problem with respect to wild rabbits, a few of us get the chance to handle them. Domestic animals do, however, suffer from diseases such as ringworm and salmonella which can be contracted by humans. So it is worth remembering to maintain normal standards of hygiene, such as washing your hands after touching any rabbit. It is some comfort to know that humans cannot catch Myxomatosis or rabbit Viral Haemorrhagic Disease.

The above, somewhat brief survey of wild rabbit behaviour has, I hope, given you an insight into the fascinating creatures we so often take for granted as we speed past them gently grazing the roadside verges, or look on as cuddly, though perhaps not overly interesting pets. Rabbits are well adapted to their lot as a highly predated species. Their physique and social behaviour are designed to increase each individual's chance of survival. The way they rear their young is, to our knowledge, unique for a species whose offspring are born so undeveloped and helpless. An interesting beast.

Part Three

WHY DOES MY RABBIT . . . ?

In the previous two parts we have discussed the need to weigh all the factors which may influence an animal's behaviour in order to understand why an animal does . . . We have seen that behaviour is the result of the interplay between an animal's genetics, experiences and state of health. We have also taken a brief excursion into the life of the wild rabbit and the A to Z of normal rabbit behaviour. We can now turn to contemplate some examples of undesirable behaviours our rabbits may display.

The strategies I suggest in the following pages should not be considered to be final or applicable to every instance of a rabbit showing a specific behaviour problem. Rather, they should be thought of as examples of behavioural therapy which have worked in practice. It is important to remember that each rabbit is an individual and each family he or she belongs to is also made up of individuals. All those concerned, human, rabbit or other, will be a product of their own genetics and experience, and consequently, much thought must be taken in the design of each therapeutic behaviour modification pro-gramme. Once a behaviourist has established the cause of the problem and possible strategies for resolution, it is often the owner who is best placed to tailor a plan of action to suit the specific situation.

The following includes a selection of questions I have been asked as a behaviourist with a special interest in rabbits. Some relate to aspects of normal rabbit behaviour which owners have found puzzling. Others refer to behaviours which are problematical and can be quite serious for rabbit and/or owner. I have also included some aspects of normal rabbit behaviour not covered in the previous section.

The questions come from owners who want to know more about their rabbits. All names have been changed to maintain confidentiality. Because behaviour therapy is a specialist area and because there may be organic factors involved, it is my belief that behaviourists should work closely with the veterinary profession. Consequently I only deal with cases which have been referred by the animal's veterinary surgeon. This is true whether I see the animal face to face or can only help via the post. In the latter case, I ask owners to complete a questionnaire and provide a video of the rabbit, its problem behaviour and its environment. I work with the veterinary surgeon and the owners who are often willing to learn more about their rabbit and to implement a behaviour modification programme, and are a pleasure to work with. Modifying an animal's behaviour is not always that easy. As with all animal training programmes, changing a rabbit's behaviour requires patience and consistency. The results can be astounding and highly rewarding. Without patience and consistency, any programme has a high chance of failure.

WHY DOES MY RABBIT . . .

A

Aggression
Rabbits are selective feeders which means they search through the grass for tasty herbs or forage. To forage itself means to 'make a roving search'. Foraging for food, chewing it and digesting it all take energy. In addition, out on the surface the rabbit is exposed to predators. Selective feeding means the rabbit will expend its energies on the food plants which are most nutritious, such as tender young shoots. It makes sense, then, for a rabbit, once he has found a tasty patch, to defend it from other rabbits, or at least from those who are subordinate to the individual concerned. In the winter when food is scarce, rabbits need to become even more selfish. A scraped patch of earth which reveals a few roots, or the bark of a young sapling, may be vigorously defended. It really is a case of possession being nine-tenths of rabbit law.

Unfortunately, when a rabbit decides to direct this aggression at the hand that feeds it, we humans get rather upset. Rabbits have sharp teeth and this aggression at dinner time is not acceptable, particularly if children are responsible for feeding their pet. Food-related aggression can result in the rabbit being rehomed or put to sleep. If we consider the situation from the rabbit's point of view, it all becomes clear and possible ways of resolving the problem can be devised.

Question

My children have a one-year-old rabbit doe called Coco. She is very sweet natured and does not mind being picked up and fussed. However, she does have a dark side to her character which comes to the fore when she is given her bowl of rabbit mix or when given something special like a piece of bread or biscuit. She then turns into a growling, biting monster and has bitten both my children and would have me if given the opportunity. For safety reasons, feeding Coco is no longer the responsibility of the children. It is no longer a daily chore, rather a contest between me and the rabbit as to whether I can open the hutch and put the food bowl down and remove my arm before Coco flies out of her bedroom and sinks her teeth into my hand. So far I have been lucky, but it is only a matter of time. She doesn't seem to be so bad when she is given hay, though she still grumbles a bit.

Answer

You have noticed that Coco's behaviour is worse over her concentrated food ration and over tasty titbits. From her point of view these are worth defending. Once the bowl is in her territory, or rather the usual place for her to be fed, then by rabbit rules it is hers and hers alone. It is important that you tackle this behaviour sooner rather than later because it could become worse as she learns that aggression gets her what she wants, namely to be left alone to eat. This behaviour could extend to her defending her hay as well, or even defending her empty food bowl when you come to take it away.

It is likely that you always put the food down in a particularly part of her hutch, or run. The first step, then, is to change the location of the food bowl regularly so that any associations with a particular place are broken down. The second step is to introduce food when Coco is elsewhere and cannot see it appearing. This is of course much easier if she has a good-sized run and hutch complex. Items such as biscuit, bread or fresh vegetables and grass can be scattered around the run, allowing Coco to forage rather than have a specific place to defend.

It is also useful to get Coco to associate your hand with the giving of pleasant food items, rather than something which deposits food and then retreats. Retreating hands appear rather like retreating subordinate rabbits. When you are handling Coco away from her hutch, feed her long pieces of grass, hay, carrot strips or some other item so she can nibble one end while you hold the other. Talk to her at the same time, giving her a special word she can learn, like 'dinner'. When she is happy with this, transfer this hand feeding to her hutch.

Concentrated rabbit food is a highly desirable item for Coco but should not form the bulk of her diet (see Anorexia, p. 92, and Diet, p. 113). Provision of commercial diet and other items can be made more interesting, and less easily defended, by the use of some lateral thinking. For example, if you put the food in a plastic ball, like those for use in a washing machine, Coco will have to nose the ball around her hutch for pieces of it to fall out. You can hang carrots and other items on a piece of string from the top of her run so she can go 'carrot bobbing'.

Agility

Question

My 12-year-old daughter is completely besotted with animals and really wants to be a vet when she grows up. She has seen on television, and at a local dog club, dogs doing agility courses, running through tunnels, over seesaws and jumps. Unfortunately, we are not in the position to own a dog but we do have a young Dwarf Lop rabbit, Smudge, which I am sure you can imagine gets a lot of tender loving care. My daughter wants to know if she can build a rabbit-sized agility course for Smudge and teach him how to complete it. Would this be all right for him?

You can hang carrots on a piece of string from the top of her run . . .

Answer

Rabbit agility is not unknown and some people even have competitions among friends to see whose rabbit can complete the course with the fewest mistakes or in the fastest time. But there are some points to consider before you start Smudge, or any other rabbit, on the road to becoming an agility champion.

While exercise is good for all of us, rabbits as well as people need to get fit gradually. You do not say how old

Smudge is or whether he has a run to exercise in. Certainly, I would not advise that adult rabbits who have been confined to a hutch are trained to agility. Confinement and lack of exercise is likely to cause weak muscles and weak bones. Jumping, especially, could cause serious damage to such a rabbit.

If, on the other hand, Smudge has had lots of opportunity to stretch to his full length and hop around and thus has good bones and muscles, then by all means set him an agility course. You will need to make the jumps very low to begin with, a bean pole resting on the ground will do, and only raise it slowly. Remember that rabbits are not natural jumpers and landing can be potentially damaging, so do keep the jumps low. For more about training do look at the trick training section on p. 180.

Agoraphobia

Rabbits are not very keen on wide open spaces. Even when out feeding in a meadow or on the roadside, wild rabbits are never more than a short sprint from the safety of a burrow. Being exposed with no access to such shelter is likely to be very stressful for a rabbit as it has no escape from potential predators.

Question
I have recently adopted from a rescue society an adorable adult Rex rabbit which I have called Harrison, even though that rather shows my age. We estimate that Harrison is at least three years old. I have had built a hutch which is attached to a large wire run (3 × 2 metres or 10 × 6 feet) in the centre of my garden which I can see from my sitting-room. I had hoped to be able to watch him enjoy his new-found freedom in his wide expanse of grass, but I have been disappointed. Harrison just sits in his hutch, though he will occasionally deign to sit on the grass, so close that he almost still has one foot inside. Does

... a retreat if he is frightened and a cool place to lie on
hot days ...

he just not like his run, or is he agoraphobic? Can I do
anything? He seems so sad.

Answer

What a lovely idea to place Harrison's run and hutch
where you can watch him from your sitting-room. I have
a mental picture of you with a glass of wine giggling over
Harrison's antics. I can understand how disappointed you
must feel, but there are things you can do to help Harrison
explore and make full use of his run.

At the moment the run is, as you put it, a wide expanse
of grass which Harrison is finding frightening to explore
more than a few centimetres (inches) away from his hutch.
It is possible that he has not had access to such a large
space before. Even if he had, open spaces need to be
treated with caution if you are a rabbit and likely to be
someone's dinner. The main problem is the lack of any
cover other than his hutch. Consequently Harrison feels
insecure if he moves too far away. This insecurity may be
heightened if there are dogs, cats or foxes which visit the
area and leave their scent, or even large birds such as
magpies which he is unused to and thus finds threaten-
ing. The problem can be solved by simply providing
Harrison with objects into which he can easily retreat. Bits

of clay drainpipe serve the purpose extremely well and are available from your local builders' merchants. The pipe needs to be big enough for Harrison to lie stretched out, so about one and a half times his body length when he is sitting relaxed. The diameter of the pipe needs to be big enough for him to enter easily, but not much more than that. You may need to place a couple of wedges on either side of the pipe to stop it moving when he goes in, or sits on top of it. Harrison will soon find the pipe has at least three uses, a retreat if he is frightened, a cool place to lie on hot days and an excellent look-out place when he sits on top of it. You do not need to restrict yourself to single pieces of drainpipe; they also come as T-pieces and L-pieces, so you could set up a system of burrows for him to use. Such a system is good for rabbits living on their own or with another rabbit or cavy. In this case you should have different-sized pipes so the cavy, or smaller rabbit, if different-sized breeds, can have its 'own' space which is private.

Having provided Harrison with his burrows, you may wish to tempt him away from his hutch by leaving tasty morsels around the run. If he enjoys being handled, then sit in the run with him and let him explore and find titbits with you there. Speak to him gently and do not make any sudden noises or movements which may confirm his suspicions that the run is rather a scary space.

These principles of providing cover, a quiet environment and positive associations with tasty titbits are equally applicable if you try to introduce Harrison, or any other rabbit, to the inside of your home, whether he is just a temporary visitor for the evening or is to become a house rabbit.

Anorexia

Rabbits stop eating and lose weight for a variety of reasons. In most cases there is a medical cause. Sadly for many rabbits, there is little that can be done for them as often owners do not realise there is a problem until it is too late. It is important to give your rabbit a weekly health check which should include weighing it and noting if there is any change. Rabbits can lose condition very fast and regular checks and prompt action can often make the difference between life and death. If you are at all worried, do not hesitate to take your rabbit to the veterinary surgeon for a check-up.

The rabbit may be suffering from some viral or bacterial infection. Parasites inside the body, for example worms, or on the skin, such as fleas and ticks, can debilitate a rabbit so that it feels too unwell to eat. A rabbit which has eaten something poisonous may also be too sick to eat properly. Poisoning or even a rapid change in diet can cause diarrhoea which can make the rabbit dehydrated. A dehydrated animal will not eat; in such a condition it needs water more than food.

Perhaps the most common cause of rabbit anorexia is malocclusion of the teeth, that is where the teeth are not aligned properly. Rabbit teeth grow continuously throughout their lives and need to be worn down every day. Under natural conditions this results from the rabbit slicing through grasses with the front teeth and the grinding action of the back teeth breaking up the grass before it is swallowed. Unfortunately, rabbits which are fed predominantly on commercial pelleted food do not use their teeth appropriately. Unlike grass which requires grinding by the molars, pellets are crushed. This crushing action does not wear down the molars fast enough to stop them becoming overgrown. In consequence they can become misaligned, so causing misalignment of the incisors as well.

Where the back teeth no longer wear each other down, they develop sharp spurs which dig into the side of the cheek or tongue causing lacerations or ulcers which are obviously very painful. Just think how you feel when you accidentally bite your tongue. For rabbits with misaligned teeth, the wounds on the tongue do not heal but are aggravated every time the rabbit chews a mouthful of food. These lacerations can become infected, adding to the rabbit's misery. Not surprisingly, the pain stops the rabbit eating.

It is often necessary for rabbits to have their front teeth clipped. However, recent work by David Crossley, a veterinarian specialising in dental issues, has shown that clipping the front teeth can, in itself, exacerbate the situation by causing the teeth to crack or forcing them to grow back into the head. This sometimes causes a blocking of the lachrymal duct (tear duct to you and me) which leads to infection in the tissues around the eye, known as conjunctivitis. Infection in this area with pasturella bacteria causes problems with the eyes and nose. It is commonly known as 'snuffles', which is often incurable. Worse still, the misaligned teeth can grow back into the eye socket causing abscesses behind the eye or in the bone of the skull. Little can be done for a rabbit in such a state, other than to put it to sleep humanely.

Clipping the front teeth will not resolve a problem totally if there are nasty, sharp spurs on the back teeth which are not attended to. It is not easy, either, to see these spurs in a rabbit which is awake. A general anaesthetic is needed to clip or rasp the back teeth. Because the teeth keep growing, the rabbit may have to undergo an operation regularly, which is not totally without risk, or have all its teeth pulled out, not a pleasant option either. Rabbits can, in fact, eat and survive without any teeth, so you may think extracting all your rabbit's teeth would at least solve the problem once and for all. But apart from ethical issues, removing all the teeth is a difficult procedure and is not always 100 per cent successful. Even a little bit of tooth tissue accidentally left behind can grow as a new tooth, and this new tooth may not grow in the right direction but try to emerge from the side of the mouth or behind an eye. The result then is usually euthanasia.

Teeth problems can occur in all rabbits, though they are often more rapidly developed in the smaller, dwarf breeds. This is because teeth in these animals grow just as quickly but, because the head is so much smaller, any misalignment will have a noticeable effect sooner. Sadly, breeding dwarf animals, whether rabbits or dogs, is always accompanied by problems.

There is an easy way to help prevent this problem. Simply make the bulk of your rabbit's diet hay or fresh grass, fruit and vegetables. If you wish to give him commercial food, do so only sparingly. This is just as important for house rabbits as it is for those kept in hutches and runs.

Remember, RABBITS EAT GRASS —and will thrive on it. Grass, either fresh or dried as hay, will provide all their nutrition and keep their teeth healthy. If you are worried that it is not very nutritious, think how big horses, cattle and even buffalo grow just by eating grass.

You may suspect that grass is not very tasty and that your rabbit will get bored. Certainly, this may be true if you buy hay made from a monoculture crop, which also may not be completely balanced. If you buy organically grown hay it will include a variety of grasses and herbs, be bursting with flavours rabbits love, be nutritionally balanced and have no potentially nasty herbicides or pesticides which may detrimentally affect your rabbit's health in the long term. My own rabbits have rarely been fed commercial food, but were given hay, fresh picked (not mown) grass, groundsel (*Senecio vulgaris*), dandelions (*Taraxacum officinale*) and carrots. I can honestly say they never had teeth problems and lived for seven years or more.

I should also add that there is some evidence of an inherited tendency to malocclusion. Do check with the breeder that there is no such problem in his stock. If there is, I suggest you buy your rabbit elsewhere.

Anthropomorphism

Anthropomorphism is when we imbue an animal with human characteristics. Rabbits have rounded heads and bodies and large eyes. These proportions are similar to those of human babies and seem to be characteristics to which we are naturally attracted and responsive. Through the process of domestication we have enhanced the 'human-like' qualities, particularly in breeds of dog which are intended first and foremost as companions, such as the Pekingese and Cavalier King Charles Spaniel. We have also enhanced them in many rabbit breeds. The droopy ears of the Lops emphasise the rounded head shape. The tiny ears of the dwarf breeds with their compact little bodies have a similar effect. The long coats of the Cashmeres and Angoras typify the 'fluffy, baby bunny'.

This is all well and good, so long as we remember that our rabbit is still a rabbit, no matter what it looks like, and we are aware of what we are doing. It is fine to consider your rabbit one of the family, a good friend and confidant, but do remember that he or she is still a rabbit, will behave like a rabbit and will need to eat an appropriate diet. Sometimes we forget this simple fact, and expect our rabbits to act the way we think they ought to do, from our human perspective. We forget the simple things such as that a rabbit is a prey animal and will have a different outlook on the world. Such anthropomorphic mistakes may be the basis of problem behaviours.

Attention seeking

Rabbits are social animals and can be rather manipulative. They can train their owners to give them attention when they are feeling left out of things. This can result in behaviour which the owner might find either amusing or a problem.

Question

I have a wonderful rabbit, a Californian called Tussle. Luckily I live in a Victorian terrace house with a garden which is completely walled. So, though Tussle is basically a house rabbit, he can have free range of the garden while we are there. Ever since he was a baby he has had a passion about laundry and would pull items from the basket and promptly sit on them. He then turned his attention to helping me remove the laundry from the machine. Now Tussle's antics have progressed to outside. When I hang the laundry out on the line he is very interested and, due to his size, can reach longer items such as sheets or trouser legs. These he grips with his teeth and pulls, as if he is playing a game of tug-of-war, hence his name. If I am not on the alert, he will also steal laundry out of the basket and disappear up the garden with it, resulting in a game of chase between him and me. This is not a problem as I find it an amusing aspect of his character, but I would be interested in any thoughts you might have as to why he does this.

Answer

It appears from your description that Tussle's behaviour has developed from an innocent curiosity to a learnt attention-seeking behaviour. When he was little, the laundry from the basket was in itself quite rewarding. Not only was it a form of play but it resulted in something nice and comfortable to sit on. He then generalised this behaviour to the washing machine, and probably got a reaction from you such as a stroke and a laugh. Now he has learnt that this is a sure-fire way of obtaining your attention, which in itself is a positive reward. The basic principles of learning theory tell us that if a behaviour has a rewarding outcome, then an animal will learn to repeat that action—precisely what Tussle has learnt.

Question

I am a single woman of mature years and I share my life with Mozart, my Miniature Lop house rabbit. Mozart happily sits on the sofa with me, listening to music while I stroke him. He loves visitors and enjoys being stroked by anyone. He cannot get enough attention. Indeed, in many ways he is the perfect companion, apart from his seeming jealousy. If I am busy washing up the dishes, or sit at my writing table for any length of time, he nips the back of my ankles. This is quite painful and extremely annoying. Do you have any suggestions?

Answer

You have rightly diagnosed Mozart's motivation for his behaviour, in that it is a means of obtaining your attention. It sounds as though Mozart is a little spoilt, and why not? However, his love of attention means that he resents it when you turn your concentration to something else like the washing-up or writing a letter. Mozart is resorting to the normal rabbit behaviour of a quick nip if other attention-seeking behaviours do not work. I would hypothesise that Mozart originally started by weaving in and out of your legs in an attempt to get you to notice him. When this did not work he tried an exploratory nip and, hey presto, it worked. Even if you only momentarily turned to him and perhaps shooed him away, he still got your attention. Nipping your ankles had a rewarding outcome, so he has learnt to repeat it. This is similar to the dog who barks when its owner makes a telephone call and the owner turns to tell the dog to be quiet. The owner has perhaps learnt that the only way to ensure peace is to stroke the dog or give it a biscuit. The dog has now trained its owner to do what it wants. And we humans like to think we are the clever ones!

In order to stop this behaviour, Mozart needs to learn that it no longer gets him what he wants. There are two ways this can be accomplished. The first is to put Mozart

Attention-seeking behaviour.

on what is technically known as an extinction schedule. This means that you extinguish his nipping behaviour by teaching him that it has no result whatsoever, in other words you should not react to his nipping. You may think that a set of rabbit incisors in your leg is not easy to ignore and I can only agree. But it can be done, if you take to wearing some short leather boots or even a pair of old wellingtons (I say old because they will probably end up with a few puncture holes). You will need to wear these not only every time you wash up or sit at your writing desk, but at other times as well, when you are stroking Mozart. Otherwise, he will learn that the boots are the discriminating cue as to when nipping will not work. Then, when you think you have the problem cured and you start washing up in your ordinary shoes, Mozart will be there nipping away just as he always did.

The second technique is to teach Mozart that nipping

has a negative, or non-rewarding outcome. Preferably, he will associate this non-reward with the nipping and not with you. The judicial use of a bit of water here can work very well. A couple of indoor plant-watering sprays will be required, one near the sink and one at your desk. When Mozart has a nip, say 'Mozart, no' firmly and immediately spray him with some water. This will do him no harm, but he is unlikely to like it. Very few rabbits like what amounts, basically, to a shower of rain. Otherwise, ignore him. Mozart will soon learn that nipping results in not only a 'No' but also getting wet. If you are consistent, and do this *every* time he nips, he will soon learn that it is not a very productive behaviour. You will also have taught him that 'No' means 'Stop whatever you are doing, or risk getting wet.' This is a very useful thing to teach a rabbit and can be used for other misdemeanours such as nibbling furniture.

Aversion
Rabbits are wary animals and they need to be: if you are a prey animal, there is rarely a chance to rectify your mistakes. A basic rabbit rule of life is, if something is strange, be aware that it may be aversive. At the same time they are also full of curiosity and will investigate their surroundings thoroughly as long as they feel secure, so it is important to introduce your rabbit to new things in a way that makes it feel safe.

Question
I am not sure if the problem I have with my house rabbit is my problem or his. I have a Dutch rabbit called Jeeves, because he looks as if he is dressed in his dinner suit. He is lots of fun, but does tend to get quite worried by change. He had an indoor kennel in my living room, but has free range of my ground-floor flat. The problem I have is that I am a frustrated interior designer and periodically I love to change my furniture around or redecorate. Every time

I do, Jeeves seems to skulk in his kennel and, if he does venture out, the slightest noise or movement starts him thumping his back legs and scurrying back to his kennel. If I have relocated his kennel, he seems even more upset. Am I being cruel in indulging my habit of changing my surroundings? What can I do to make it less traumatic for Jeeves?

Answer
This is a wonderful example of the difference between us primates and many other species of animal. Most animals do not take easily to change in their surroundings, perhaps particularly a prey species like a rabbit. The rabbit's survival depends on intimate knowledge of its surroundings so that it can rapidly run down familiar routes to escape a predator. You may have noticed, when on a walk in the country, distinct rabbit runs through the undergrowth, which are highways back to the safety of the warren.

When we move the furniture in a room, it is easy for us to see the new layout and to realise that it is still the same room. After all, we have a view from above, so to speak. But from the rabbit's perspective the room is completely different. In order to understand what I mean, lie down on the floor and look at the room from rabbit height. If you have put new covers on the furniture or repainted, the room doesn't even smell the same, which is even worse from a rabbit's point of view. How very confusing and worrying for Jeeves. It is not surprising that he remains in the comparative safety of his kennel with its familiar smells. When you move the kennel too, he is even more disorientated as he is unclear how to get back to it.

You have commented that during this time he seems to be particularly sensitive to sudden noises and movements and resorts to thumping and retreating to his kennel. From Jeeves's point of view the world has changed;

what may have been an unthreatening noise in his old environment may herald danger in the new. He is not going to take any chances, so he thumps a warning and runs for cover.

If you are like me, then changing a room happens in one fell swoop. Chairs and tables are moved around, rugs relocated and ornaments swopped. Unfortunately, this is not rabbit friendly. I do not think you should stop indulging your love of change, but do it in such a way that Jeeves can feel secure. This means changing things gradually, allowing Jeeves to explore and become familiar with one aspect of the new layout at a time. Where possible, do not move his kennel, but if you need to then do it gradually, moving it only a foot or so at a time. It may take you several days to shift your room around, but think of the pleasure of anticipating the final result and of having a secure and contented bunny to share it with.

B

Babies

Question
I have never had a rabbit before. However, I am now in a position to give a rabbit a good home. I would like to buy a baby one and have set my heart on a Miniature Lop. I have seen plenty in pet shops, but am not sure this is the right place from which to buy one. Could you please advise? I may wish to breed rabbits of my own and would like some guidance about how to prepare them for a new home.

Answer
Personally, I do not like to see animals being sold in pet shops. I think it is better for the animal only to have to go through the difficult process of rehoming once, from its place of birth to a new, permanent home. This is true whether it is a cat, dog, rabbit or any other species. Pet shops can rarely give you reliable information about the origins of their stock. For example, you have no idea if the parents were healthy and good-tempered. We know that animals are influenced by their genetics and early surroundings. It is often reported that young rabbits bought from pet shops suffer from scouring, or chronic diarrhoea. This is likely to be due in part to diet change as well as to the stresses involved in being transported to

and living in, a noisy pet-shop environment. No, it is far preferable to buy an animal direct from its breeder and for you to go and pick it up. Do not buy a pet which is delivered, as you do not know where it has come from. With the increasing popularity of the rabbit, it is likely that there will be an increase in unscrupulous breeders out to make a profit. This has already happened in the dog world with the development of 'puppy farms' where puppies are bred in awful conditions to be sold to the unwitting public.

If you know someone who has a rabbit which is a pleasure to own, ask them for the name of the breeder. Otherwise contact your local veterinary surgeon, the British Houserabbit Association or the British Rabbit Council. Do go and visit the breeder before you make your choice. Ask to see all the stock, not just the litter they are selling. Do the rabbits look relaxed and well cared for? Remember that shiny clean cages may not be the most important thing. Are the rabbits jumpy when a stranger is in the shed or room? If so then it is likely they have not been handled much and the kitten you take home may be very nervous and not make a good pet. How old are the kittens? It is advisable to buy one around six or seven weeks of age, which has already been well handled.

A young animal, especially one like the rabbit which is social, must develop a species and an individual identity. This process is known as socialisation. If the animal is exposed to members of more than one species during the sensitive period for socialisation then a multiple species identity can develop. This is of importance to companion animal species which are expected to cohabit with humans, their own and, possibly, other species.

It is not known at what age the rabbit is most sensitive to being socialised to humans. It is likely to be earlier than with cats or dogs, given that overall development is completed in a much shorter time span. Socialisation in the dog and cat seems to be equated with the time the animal starts to leave the nest, which would be around two to three weeks of age for the rabbit. For her Master's project on the Southampton Companion Animal Behaviour Course, Simone der Weduwen conducted a study to attempt to identify this period for the rabbit. While her results have not been able to establish a clear socialisation period, there is evidence to suggest that handling kittens between four and six weeks of age helps them become accustomed to people and, accordingly, be better-adjusted pets, more easily handled.

If you are planning to breed a litter of rabbits, or buy a kitten, then check that the kittens have been socialised. They should be gently handled on emergence from the nest. Some bedding in the nest should also be handled at this point so that scent is transferred, thereby reducing any chance of rejection by the doe. Indeed, where possible, namely with a friendly doe, she too should be handled. It is important that the weight of the animal is fully supported and that handling does not cause pain. Remember not to squeeze the thorax or abdominal area and take particular care with kittens and dwarf breeds.

Handling should be done by several people, of both sexes, and particularly the future owners. A rabbit which has been handled only by men, for example, is likely not to recognise women and children as familiar; it would be nervous of them and may show fear aggression (see p. 125). Men, women and children sound different and emit different odours and are thus easily distinguished from each other.

Sounds that rabbits may meet in their new home should also be introduced. Gentle background 'muzak' of washing machines, doorbells, dogs barking, children laughing, babies crying, etc., can all make the transition to their new home less traumatic. Putting objects in the kittens' pen for them to explore is also a good idea. Again, as with Jeeves's story (p. 100), the kittens should not be swamped with novelty, just one or two things at a time.

These objects can be anything which is not harmful, such as pieces of wood, old boxes, solid balls or articles which have been handled or kept at the new owner's house so the smell of the new home is introduced. The idea is to get them used to novelty.

C

Canker
See Head shaking, p. 135.

Cats
Cats and rabbits are not natural friends. As the pet-food manufacturers have noticed, cats eat rabbits. That does not mean they cannot live happily alongside a pet rabbit, whether it is kept in the garden or in the house. It should still never be forgotten that cats are predators; it is unwise to leave cat and rabbit together unattended. This is less of a problem if the rabbit, when adult, is bigger than the cat. I would certainly suggest that cat owners go for the larger breeds of rabbit rather than miniature or dwarf breeds.

Introducing your cat to your rabbit, or vice versa, really does require the use of a pen or indoor kennel. This can contain either cat or rabbit while the other is left to wander around. Provision of tasty titbits for both animals will also help them make positive associations with the presence of the other. As Sarah Heath explains in *Why Does My Cat . . . ?*, cats are very scent orientated. It is a good idea to rub your rabbit gently with a clean cloth and then rub it on to the cat's back and flanks. This way you will transfer the rabbit's scent on to the cat which will help the latter accept the former more easily. The same process can be done in reverse so the rabbit gets the opportunity to become acquainted with the scent of your cat. Cats and rabbits can

Rabbits may chase cavies . . .

become firm friends, as can rabbits and dogs. It is not unusual to see a cat sharing its basket with the family rabbit, gently washing its ears. I have even heard of a cat who chose the family rabbit's hutch as the place in which to give birth to her kittens, with the rabbit still in residence.

Chasing
Rabbits chase each other as part of the courtship ritual, in territorial disputes and, apparently, for the sheer joy of it. A rabbit can also learn that this is an appropriate way of interacting with a member of another species. This may take the form of chasing its owner's feet or even playing with the family dog. I have a friend whose rabbit, aptly named Funbun, used to be chased down the length of the garden, only to turn round at the end and proceed to chase the dog back up again. This would continue for several minutes at a time, to the delight of onlookers and, seemingly, to the participants.

Chasing may not always be so innocent. If you have rabbits housed together or with a cavy then it is important to make sure this behaviour is not based in aggression or misplaced courtship. Often such chasing will happen when two rabbits are first introduced as they sort out their relationship. The rabbit may also chase a newly introduced cavy for the same reason. This can be quite stressful to the cavy and the rabbit, though the situation should settle down quite quickly. If not, it may be these animals are not suited to each other. Be sure to provide escape places or hidy-holes not only during the period of introduction but for the whole of the animals' lives. Chasing and increased aggression can result simply from two animals being cooped up together for long periods with no means of getting out of each other's sight. It happens in the best of families. We all need time away from even our nearest and dearest.

Chewing

Question
I have kept rabbits for most of my life, but they have always lived outside in their hutch and run. I had never thought of having one as a house rabbit and am rather intrigued by the idea. I have recently lost my last rabbit, at the age of ten, and would like to keep her successor indoors. However, I have one major worry, my furniture. I have a few pieces of antique furniture, a couple of chairs and a chest of drawers, and I know rabbits love to chew wood. Over the years I have had to patch up the hutch and run where the little terrors have nibbled away. I would be heartbroken if my furniture was treated in a similar fashion, much as I love rabbits. Is there anything I can do, or should I abandon the idea of a house rabbit?

Answer
No, do not abandon the idea. There are several issues which need to be considered when introducing a rabbit to life indoors (see House training, p. 136, Indoor rabbits, p. 138, Pica, p. 166, and Trick training, p. 181). The safest answer with regard to your furniture is to place it in a room to which the rabbit will not have access. If this is not convenient, make sure you supervise your rabbit's activities when he is free running, until he understands more about the house rules. If he approaches the relevant

items of furniture, say your rabbit's name and 'No' in a firm voice. If he takes no notice, squirt him with some water from your ever handy indoor plant spray. To learn effectively that these bits of furniture are out of bounds, your rabbit must be told 'No' *every* time he approaches them (see Attention seeking, p. 96). It is not as easy as it sounds, so there is a back-up plan.

Wrap some clingfilm around the legs of your furniture and tie some cloth on top of that. Spray the cloth with a proprietary chew repellent designed to deter kittens and puppies. Take care not to get any spray on the furniture itself. Renew the spray daily and continue this until the rabbit loses interest. This can be used for other items too.

Children

It has long been held that rabbits are the ideal pets for children. I wonder. Of course we first have to consider what we actually mean by children. I do not think any child should be given full responsibility for the maintenance of a pet; they should always be under the guidance of their parents. Obviously younger children will need more hands-on help. Older children also need to be reminded of their responsibility. A pet quickly loses pride of place in the child's interest, taking second place to playing football, going out with the girls or dressing up for the boys. We have to remember that rabbits are long-lived pets.

If children are really going to benefit from the lessons learnt by caring for a pet, they must do so throughout its life. This can encompass some awkward years of human development. I obtained one of my rabbits, Nomad, when I was 11 years old and she lived until I was 22. It would be a lie to say there were never times when I felt that looking after her and my other pets (which included mice, cavies, a sheep, chickens and tortoises) was really more of a chore than a pleasure, and one I resented. This was especially true when in my teens. After all, I had far more important things to do on my Saturdays than spend half the day cleaning them all out, but my parents made it quite clear who was responsible for the welfare of the animals. When I broke my leg, though, and later when I was at university, my mother kindly looked after Nomad and the menagerie, which taught me a lesson in sharing and appreciation of others' help. It was lovely to be able to come home to my rabbit who was always pleased to see me. Caring for a pet can help a child learn about responsibility, etc., but only if the parents are going to be involved. Animals cannot magically teach the children by themselves.

Children can be a pleasure but they often take things past the point of pleasure, whether intentionally or unwittingly. The baby who eagerly grips your finger is sweet, but it is not so delightful when the grip is transferred to your hair, beard or moustache. Older children run around, trip, fall, laugh, cry and scream, in pain and delight. They are really rather unpredictable; for a rabbit, they can be very frightening. It is important, then, that children are taught how to handle their rabbits. Children under the age of seven or eight should not be left unsupervised with a rabbit. They rarely have an understanding of their own strength and can unintentionally cause pain to a rabbit by enthusiastically squeezing it in a loving hug. This is even more likely if the rabbit is young or of a small breed. If you are intending to have rabbits and young children together I would suggest a more robust, placid breed like a French Lop, British Giant or Vienna Blue. These also tend to be too big for a child to pick up and accidentally drop. If your rabbit is living outside, try to provide it with a run which is big enough for rabbit and child to sit or lie about in. My mother built me some amazing rabbit pens under an old lean-to. They were very large and each contained a hutch raised off the ground. There was plenty of room for me to sit reading a book with a rabbit on my lap and a cavy nibbling around my feet.

Chins

It may seem that rabbits have several chins. In fact, like you and me, they only have one, that piece of flesh covering their jaw. The skin here is quite ticklish and a bit lumpy due to the underlying scent gland (see Marking, p. 152). It can also be quite damp, especially in unneutered bucks, whose scent gland is very active. However, a permanently wet chin may well indicate a sore mouth as a result of teeth problems. Ulceration of the mouth causes the rabbit to salivate excessively. A wet chin may also be caused by a weeping abscess, which may or may not be treatable, depending on its location. If the abscess is located in the bone of the jaw or cheek bones then it is unlikely that your rabbit can be given any long-term treatment. If it is more superficial, a course of antibiotics should do the trick.

Rabbits, particularly older does, have several folds of skin just below their chin which are reminiscent of the double and treble chins seen on old seaside postcards. These folds provide the female with fur to line a nest. Unfortunately, they can also be the site of bacterial infection. If they get damp it is not easy for the fur to dry. The folds provide a nice warm, moist home in which bacteria can proliferate and infect the skin. So do check that your rabbit is kept in clean, dry conditions and provided with water in a bottle and not a bowl.

Cleaning

See Maggots, p. 150.

D

Den

At the risk of being repetitive, I will state once again that rabbits are prey animals and require a safe place to which they can retreat and where they can feel relaxed. This is their den. It could be the sleeping quarters of their hutch or an indoor kennel. It should be fairly dark. If indoors, place the kennel in a quiet corner and partially cover it with a cloth. It is a good idea to teach children that if the rabbit is in its den, it is to be left alone. The same rule goes for adults. That way the rabbit can decide when it has had enough of children's or adults' attention.

Diet

Just like cats, dogs, horses and people, rabbits can detect taste and will have preferences for certain foods. Sometimes these preferences are quite odd, such as Rocky the rabbit's love of fried bacon and Fluff's partiality for pizza. Many rabbits will enjoy a piece of chocolate, but it is not terribly good for them. As with humans, chocolate and other sweet things can cause rotting of the teeth. Unlike us, rabbits do not clean their teeth, so they should not be given sweet things to eat, or food which can lodge between their teeth and cause decay. Obviously you will want to treat your rabbit, but it is sensible to give it treats which will not be detrimental to its health, and then in moderation. Even apparently harmless items can do substantial damage if given in quantity. Apples and other fruits, for instance, contain a lot of sugars and can cause tooth decay. Sweet biscuits and bread also contain sugar and should be given only in small quantities and infrequently, if at all.

Question
I have three rabbits, two neutered males which live in a hutch-run outside which can be moved around the garden. The third, a French Lop doe, is a house rabbit. I am very confused about what I should be feeding them. Do they need different diets and if so, what? There is an increasing variety of commercial rabbit foods and 'treats' on the market. I also understand that some of the plants I grow in my garden may be poisonous to rabbits. Does this mean I should not let my garden rabbits out in their run?

Answer
I am going to consider your question in three parts. The first is to clarify your query as to whether house rabbits require a different diet from those living outdoors. The answer is simply, no. But your indoor rabbit may require less food as she will be living in a warmer environment and will not be using up as much energy to keep warm as will the two boys outside.

The second part of your question concerns what sort of food you should be giving them as their main diet and what treats are suitable. Quite honestly, the best form of food as their main diet is grass or hay which has not been treated with herbicides or pesticides. With respect to your two garden rabbits, moving their hutch-run around the lawn has many benefits. From the rabbits' point of view it allows them the opportunity to graze and select tasty bits from your lawn. This allows them to feed normally and gives them a suitable, natural way of filling up their day. From your point of view, it means you get your lawn neatly mown and fertilised by their nitrogen-rich droppings with very little effort on your part. I had an uncle once who kept geese for the same lawn-mowing purpose. (They were also very effective 'watchdogs', not a role a rabbit is terribly good at.)

Commercial rabbit feeds are intended to provide a balanced diet for your pet. However, rabbits can be quite fastidious eaters as they are naturally selective feeders. This means that they may not eat everything in their bowl but only the bits they prefer. Because of this rabbit habit, if you are going to feed a commercial diet, then one in the form of pellets is preferable as each mouthful is nutritionally balanced. But I will emphasise, yet again, that the bulk of their diet needs to be hay or grass so that the rabbits can keep their teeth in trim by slicing and grinding and so avoid all the potentially horrific results of misaligned teeth (see Anorexia, p. 92).

Finally, yes, you are right: some plants are poisonous to rabbits and should be avoided. A list of some of the more common species are given in Appendix 1. If you are unsure about any plant you may have in your garden or are considering adding to your collection, do ask your veterinary surgeon, who should have access to the most recent edition of the reference book on the subject of poisons and veterinary medicine. Obviously, if your rabbit looks unwell or starts to dribble excessively, then do not waste any time, take it straight to your vet.

Digging
There is no way around this; rabbits are inveterate diggers. Given half a chance they will dig holes in your carpets, your lawn and your flower beds. My first rabbit, Thumper, did not make himself terribly popular with my mother the day he decided to dig a hole in the mattress of a bed. What made it worse was that I hadn't noticed, too busy reading a book beside him. Thumper was sitting quite happily in his newly made den. Ah, the mistakes of the beginner rabbit owner are many—and rarely repeated, we hope.

Because digging is a natural behaviour, for which rabbits

are strongly motivated, it seems only reasonable that we give them the opportunity to do so. If your rabbit is outside, where possible provide it with a digging pit. Ideally, this would be quite large, but even an area big enough for your rabbit to get in and turn round will be appreciated. It can be filled with a mixture of sand and earth (see Warrens, p. 190). A children's sandpit is ideal for all rabbits, house rabbits being given supervised digging time in it.

Indoors, rabbits tend to dig in dark, secret corners and behind furniture. This often goes undetected until you move the sofa to look for that item you lost two weeks earlier. Then, horror, you find tufts of carpet scattered everywhere. Unless you are to keep an eagle eye on your rabbit all the time (remember Thumper and the mattress), I suggest you take precautionary steps to save your carpet. Tack or glue a carpet offcut on to a piece of hardboard and place it securely in the spot your rabbit has decided to dig. Alternatively, provide the rabbit with his own digging chamber, a wooden or cardboard box lined with carpet and perhaps stuffed with hay. Rabbits also like to dig tunnels, this means they dig the end wall at a more vertical angle. Securely wedging a piece of carpet-covered hardboard between two pieces of furniture can provide your indoor rabbit with an artificial tunnel to dig. The same thing can be achieved for outside rabbits by wedging the hardboard vertically between two clay drain pipes. This forms an artificial dividing wall, which the rabbit can scrabble at to his heart's content.

Dogs

Question
I have a two-year-old Collie dog who is pretty relaxed and well behaved. I would like to have a house rabbit. How should I introduce the rabbit to the dog so that they will be friends? The problem is my dog loves to chase wild rabbits when he goes on a walk.

Answer

Dogs and rabbits can live together quite happily, but introductions need to be conducted with care and patience. The first thing to do is to teach your dog the word 'leave'. This command basically means 'Leave the rabbit (or whatever) because it really is not that interesting; come to me, I am far more interesting'. The leave command should be given in a pleasant, calm voice so as not to excite the dog even further. When the dog looks at you, reward it with praise or a titbit. For details on teaching this command, please see Appendix 2.

Once your dog understands this command with respect to other objects, toys and food, and enjoys obeying it, then is the time to obtain your rabbit. But first you need to be prepared, to make sure you have a dog-proof indoor kennel or rabbit pen and lots of pleasant treats for both your rabbit and dog. The plan is to enable both animals to make positive associations with the presence of the other.

Make your indoor kennel a pleasant place for your rabbit to be, with a comfortable box to give it some privacy, plenty of hay and a water bottle. Give your new rabbit a day or two in the room without the dog so it can get used to household noises and the presence of the human family. You can also use this time to tempt your rabbit with various titbits to see what it really likes. This is also the time to introduce the rabbit and dog to each other's scent by letting them sniff cloths that have been wiped over the other (see cats p. 107).

Make your initial introduction at a time when your dog is comfortably tired, perhaps after a good walk. Bring him into the room on a loose lead and let him sniff the cage, then get him to lie down quietly near the cage for a titbit or a treat such as a hide chew. Praise him gently while he is quiet. If he starts to get excited around the rabbit's kennel, then quietly say your leave command and get him settled again. After a few minutes take your dog out of the room for something pleasant and distracting such as his dinner.

After a couple of days of several short introductions, then, still with the dog on the lead, let the rabbit out of the cage. Continue as before, distracting your dog if he gets too excited. Most dogs quickly learn that the rabbit is really not a very interesting playmate and that chewing a hide bone is more rewarding.

If you are introducing a puppy to a rabbit, it is useful to get the puppy used to an indoor kennel and to teach it the leave command. Then you can introduce your house rabbit to the puppy, with the puppy ensconced in the kennel. The procedure of using the leave command and getting your puppy or adult dog to lie down can also be used to introduce them to pet rabbits kept in hutches and runs in the garden.

If you suggest to your dog when on a walk that there are 'RABBITS' and away he goes, then use a different word when talking about your pet bunny. In my own dog, Ba's case, I use the word 'bunny' for non-chasable rabbits and 'rabbit' for those in fields. I hasten to add that he is far too slow to catch rabbits and merely gives them a bit of aerobic exercise.

The suggestions above can be applied to most dogs, the only major exception being ex-racing greyhounds who have spent their whole working life being praised for chasing rabbit-like objects. If you are planning to have such a dog and rabbit together then do make the introductions with care. Whatever the breed, it is not advisable to leave a dog and rabbit together unattended as the dog may accidentally injure the rabbit in play, or natural instincts may just take over.

E

Enrichment

Research has shown that having too little to do can be just as stressful as having too much to do. A major aspect of animal welfare has been to try to find ways of improving the lives of animals kept on farms, in zoos and in laboratories. To date little of this has percolated into the pet world, though much of it is applicable. For example, cages for laboratory rabbits have changed dramatically and are very rabbit friendly, being quite large with different levels and compartments enabling animals to be housed in pairs or groups.

The standard rabbit hutch sold in pet shops is too small and really rather boring, single storeyed with a small sleeping area and slightly larger living area. This is all many rabbits can look forward to for the whole of their lives. Rabbit fanciers often keep their rabbits in stacks of cages, one on top of the other. The rabbits may see little more than their home cage, travelling box and table in the show ring. Rabbits kept for meat tend not to be given much room and are often kept on perforated floors through which their faeces can drop, so making cleaning easier. Indeed, the traditional way of keeping pet rabbits stems from the requirements of the commercial rabbit breeder, whether for meat, fur or fancy. I hope that the current changes in the way we think of rabbits and what we now know of their behaviour will percolate extensively through

... think up new ways of entertaining your rabbit.

both the commercial and the pet worlds. Most pet owners will say they like their rabbit, if not love it, and wish it no ill. Sadly, that does not mean they understand their rabbit; they tend to follow the advice given by 'professionals', much of which has not changed for over a hundred years.

We can make our rabbits' lives more interesting, and so make our rabbits themselves more interesting creatures for us to keep and enjoy.

The sterile environment provided by most cages and runs can be enriched very easily and cheaply. It is also fun to think up new ways of entertaining your rabbit. Provision of pipes for rabbits to sit in/stand on (see Agoraphobia, p. 90), ledges, tree stumps, logs to chew, hay in a hayrack and suspended items of food such as apple twigs and carrots can all serve to enrich the environment. You can enhance their mental stimulation by adding novel objects such as cardboard boxes, toilet roll tubes, or a hard plastic ball from time to time. Toys designed for cats, such as cat activity suites, comprising ramps and tubes, or cat balls which have a bell, and the wooden or hard plastic toys designed for parrots can also be suitable for your rabbit. Do ensure that any items such as twigs and branches have not been treated with pesticides, varnished or preserved in any way. If you are in doubt as to whether a toy may be toxic to your rabbit, ask the retailer or contact the manufacturer. Also, look out for small bits of plastic which the rabbit may swallow. Rabbits love chewing yoghurt pots and plastic flower pots, but I suggest they do so only when you are there to supervise.

Remember that if your rabbit has lived in a less stimulating environment, introduction of change should be done gradually.

Enurination
I have in the bathroom of my home a cartoon by Guy Troughton, from my book *Rabbits and Hares,* of a male rabbit spraying a doe with urine. The doe has a look of bliss on her face and the bubble above her head reads 'He loves me'.

It makes me smile every time I see it, but thankfully I have never had to live with a spraying rabbit.

Question
I have a magnificent, unneutered male rabbit, called Beau. He is an English and has spots along his flanks and a stripe down his back. He really is handsome. While I love him dearly, I am not enamoured by his habit of rushing past me at speed and liberally spraying me with urine. He seems to do this at the most inopportune moments, such as when I am getting ready to go out for the evening. Any ideas? He does not do this to anyone else in the household, much to my husband's amusement. Thankfully he has not done it to guests, not even the vicar.

Answer
As Beau seems to be directing this behaviour only to you, it appears that you are his chosen mate. As you say he is particularly inclined to do this when you are going out, it may be triggered by your perfume, assuming you do not always wear perfume when you are not going out. Perfumes contain real or synthetic substances which mimic the pheromones we emit when sexually aroused. I have also heard of a rabbit who only sprayed his female owner at certain times during her menstrual cycle. This

Thankfully he has not done it to guests, not even
the vicar.

spraying is hormonally driven and there is only one potential cure, I am afraid, which is to have Beau neutered.
This should dramatically decrease the likelihood of him
spraying, if not stop it altogether. Of course, you may
wish to experiment with the perfume idea and put your
perfume on after you have left the house. Alternatively,
put Beau in his indoor kennel before you get ready to go
out. But of course he may be somewhat frustrated at not
being able to express his desires, so perhaps neutering
would be kinder.

As an aside, I should point out that some females also
spray, although it is a predominantly male behaviour.
Again, neutering can substantially reduce this behaviour.

Euthanasia
There is one guaranteed fact of life, which is that it does
not go on for ever. Whether your rabbit dies at home or
has to be put to sleep by the veterinary surgeon, you may
well feel upset. That is perfectly normal, and you should
allow yourself to grieve over the loss of the companion

which brought you so much pleasure during his or her life. You may wish to commemorate your rabbit's life by burying it in the garden or having it cremated and either burying or spreading the ashes. Your veterinary surgeon can arrange to have your rabbit cremated and the ashes returned in a little casket.

Most of us need to talk to someone who understands how we feel at such a time. We may feel embarrassed talking to friends or even family, or feel they do not understand. In that case, you may wish to contact the Befriender's service. This is a voluntarily run support group for owners who have lost their pets either literally or through death and need an understanding ear. Your veterinary surgeon should have details, or contact the Society for Companion Animal Studies (see the addresses at the end of this book).

We often forget that animals, too, form attachments. You may not be the only one missing your departed rabbit. Your rabbit's cage-mate or the family dog or cat may pine and appear rather depressed and not be interested in food. This seems to be worse if the departed rabbit has just disappeared, from their point of view. It is a kindness to let the other animals see the body. They may spend some time licking it before they realise it will not respond. If your remaining pets do seem to pine, try to rekindle their interest in the world with some extra attention, favourite titbits, games or, for dogs, walks.

Excitement

Rabbits can be startled very easily. This is true for all rabbits, but even more so for those which have been kept in fairly unstimulating environments and thus have a low threshold for novelty. Given the space, a startled rabbit will run back to a place of safety. If it is unable to do so and feels trapped, it may panic and injure itself. This could happen, for instance, to a rabbit cornered by well-intentioned but misguided noisy children. Alternatively, it may feel threatened by an unusually violent thunderstorm, or a visitation from a noisy, un-rabbit-proofed dog. The rabbit may suddenly keel over and die of a heart attack or, in its attempts to escape, it may throw itself around the walls of its hutch or try to leap out of its pen, perhaps landing awkwardly and breaking its back. If caught while so excited, the rabbit may kick out violently with its back legs, again risking breaking its back. Many breaks occur just in front of the pelvis and are caused by the rabbit kicking against a solid object. Of course bones are more likely to break if they are weak or deformed, as happens with rabbits kept in confined areas such as hutches so small that they are unable to stretch out fully or move freely. In the long term such conditions cause deformity of the spine. Sadly, I suspect that is the case with the vast majority of rabbits kept as pets.

The solution is multifaceted. Introduce your rabbit to a variety of sounds and objects, so it is not so easily startled. Handle it frequently and gently. Be quiet and move slowly around your rabbit. Give it a proper diet and plenty of space so it can grow properly and remain in tip-top condition. And enjoy a long and happy relationship with your pet.

Fear aggression
Frightened rabbits will take one of three courses of action. The first option is to freeze. They may crouch down to stay out of sight, or just remain still in an attempt to avoid attracting the attention of a potential predator, many of which, such as dogs and cats, are stimulated to chase by movement and cannot notice an immobile rabbit. If the predator comes too close, the rabbit will flee, bolting towards the nearest hole. This second option is known as the 'flight response'. If the rabbit cannot flee, because it is caught in a net or cornered in a hutch, for example, then it will resort to aggression, the 'fight response'.

Question
I recently obtained a young Dwarf Lop buck rabbit for my son Sam's twelfth birthday. He has always wanted a rabbit and we felt he was now old enough to take responsibility for the care of a pet of his own. I purchased the rabbit, known as Sloppy, when he was 12 weeks old from the gentleman who bred him. He seemed a nice, quiet friendly rabbit and I looked forward to seeing my son and his new friend together.

However, the story has not turned out quite as hoped. Sloppy has been kept in a hutch which is attached to a good-sized run. He has free access to this during the day, but is locked in his hutch at night. I have never had any problem picking him up or handling him, but he hates my son and wife with a vengeance. If they put their hands in his hutch he will lunge at them and, if possible, bite them. More recently, he managed to inflict substantial damage on my son. The boy went to put Sloppy away in his hutch. The rabbit was under the hutch and Sam lay down and reached in to get him. As he did so, Sloppy pounced on his arm, bit hard and did not let go. At the same time, Sloppy kicked the arm with his back legs causing multiple lacerations. We can all see there is a friendly, sweet-natured side to Sloppy's character and we would like to give him a chance. Why is he like this and is there anything we can do? He is now ten months old. Is it too late?

Answer

The selective aggression shown by Sloppy suggests he was not adequately socialised during the first few weeks of his life. It is possible that he had not had much, if any, handling by women or children when at his breeder's. If so, then he probably does not recognise women and children as familiar, and consequently is afraid of them.

Sloppy has also learnt that he cannot escape from the hutch-run and that freezing in the presence of humans only results in him being handled. So aggression has become his appropriate coping strategy. By showing aggression he ensures the removal of the frightening stimulus, the hand.

You ask if you can do anything to resolve his behaviour and the answer, I am happy to say, is yes. It will require patience on the part of your wife and Sam. You will need a soft baby brush, a piece of dowelling about 45 cm (18 in) long and lots of Sloppy's favourite titbits. You will also need to agree on a cue word for Sloppy such as 'lift' which means he is about to be picked up and can prepare himself. Being lifted can in itself be quite frightening and is something most rabbits do not enjoy. It must feel like

Attach the baby brush to a piece of dowel.

being whizzed up in a speeding lift or taking off in a small aeroplane, quite disturbing when you feel as if you have left your stomach behind.

Attach the baby brush to a piece of dowel. When Sloppy is in his hutch, or preferably in his run, start to stroke him gently around his head, gradually along the back and around his chest. All the time talk to him quietly saying, 'Sloppy, lift.' At the same time let Sloppy tuck into a mound of his favourite goodies such as dandelion leaves. If he turns round to bite the brush, just carry on brushing, perhaps moving back up towards his head. This way Sloppy will learn that biting has no effect. Repeat this procedure for short periods of only a few minutes over and over again.

Over a period of several days, Sloppy will become more relaxed and you can start to shorten the dowel and eventually remove it and hold the brush. Soon enough you will be able to discard the brush and stroke him with your hand. Gradually begin to lift his hindquarters gently a few centimetres (inches) off the ground and put them back down. Once he is happy with this, start to entice him on to your lap with his titbits. The final stage is to hold him, gently but securely, when he is on your lap, and lift him.

It is important to hold a rabbit so that its body weight is supported and it can feel secure. It will often prefer to have its head tucked under the crook of your arm. With a small or skittish rabbit, cover its eyes with your hand, making sure you support it between its front legs with your fingers. Large rabbits will need to be supported by a whole hand under their chest. The body of the rabbit should be supported by the length of your other arm and held firmly but gently against your body. If in doubt, ask your local veterinary surgeon or an experienced rabbit person to show you how. Remember, a rabbit's ears are not designed to be carrying handles.

Fighting
Rabbits fight; this is a fact of life. If a rabbit fight does break out in an enclosed space where neither individual can get away, it can be very bloody and fatal for one if not both individuals concerned. This does not mean that rabbits should be kept alone. It just means a little thought needs to be given to who lives with whom. The golden rules to follow are: do not keep unneutered males together, do not keep unneutered females together and, unless you want lots of kittens, do not keep an unneutered male with an unneutered female.

Neutered male rabbits, especially if litter brothers, can live together quite amicably. Also a neutered pair, a male and female, can enjoy each other's company for many a long year. The female of the species is not always quite so accommodating, and two females, even if neutered, will tend to have the occasional squabble resulting in some fur flying. The important thing to remember, whatever the pairing, is to make sure the rabbits have plenty of room and lots of hidy-holes. Also realise that, like us, rabbits have different personalities and, no matter what you think, one rabbit may simply dislike another.

It is not really advisable to keep more than two rabbits together as, inevitably, a hierarchy will develop and you will have to keep a careful watch to ensure no one is getting excessively bullied.

Fly strike
See Maggots, p. 150.

Friskiness
I am often asked, 'Why does my rabbit suddenly rush madly around his run?' or, in the case of house rabbits, 'around the room'. This mad five minutes tends to happen early in the morning or in the evening, when rabbits are naturally more active, being crepuscular creatures. It is also more obvious in young rabbits who are still agile and full of the joys of living. That is not to say that older rabbits do not indulge in such mad moments, they just do so for less time and with not quite so much verve. Rather like me, really.

It is biologically adaptive for rabbits to keep themselves fit, as a fit rabbit is more likely to stay alive. A quick burst of aerobic exercise helps. Of course, you could always assume the rabbit is just enjoying itself. It certainly seems that way. Until we can speak rabbit, or find Dr Dolittle, who can say?

Fur plucking
Fur plucking is a predominantly female activity, though it has been reported, rarely, by owners of male rabbits. The female pulls fur from her chest, belly and flanks and uses it to line the nest she prepares for her kittens. This will happen near the end of the pregnancy and also in cases where the female has a false pregnancy. Fur pulling is a normal maternal behaviour and really nothing to

worry about. However, if your doe has a tendency to false pregnancies, it may be advisable to have her neutered.

Fur pulling
Whilst plucking fur may be a normal, hormonally driven behaviour, extensive pulling of fur from the body may indicate a problem.

Question
My rabbit, Trouble, should really be called Scruffy. She is quite bald in patches along her flanks and her back. She spends inordinate amounts of time rubbing herself along the hutch door and pulling hunks of fur out. At first I thought she was just moulting, but this seems to continue for months on end.

Answer
Rabbits do moult and are inclined to look fairly scruffy during this period. However, in Trouble's case this does not seem to be the problem. I suggest a trip to the vet is in order. Rabbits can suffer from a variety of skin parasites including fleas and mites. Ear mites infest the ears, causing the rabbit to shake its head and rub its ears. Another type of mite can live in the rabbit's skin. These mites burrow under the skin surface, causing the rabbit a lot of irritation. You will see patches of fur loss and scurfy skin where the mites are active. All such diseases need treating by your veterinary surgeon, as drops or washes from the pet shop will not be effective against these mites. Do not be tempted to use substances designed for use on cats and dogs. They may well be unsafe to use on your rabbit. Another cause of fur pulling, particularly in longer-coated breeds, is tangled mats which cause the animal discomfort. It is important to check your rabbit carefully at least weekly for any such problems (see Grooming, p. 132).

G

Greeting

While rabbits are social animals, they are also small prey animals and as a consequence their behaviour is quite subtle. Rabbits do not go in for the extravagant greeting displays we see in dogs, nor are they even as outgoing as the cat which calls to you as it comes in through the cat flap, just to make sure you are ready to receive it and stroke it when it decides to come and find you. But rabbits can be just as loving and just as demanding in their own quiet, demure way.

Tame and well-handled rabbits will come to the edge of their hutch or indoor kennel to greet you. They may well utter a low purring noise and, given the opportunity, will chin your shoes to reinstate you as one of the family (see Marking, p. 152).

... given the opportunity, they will chin your shoes ...

Grooming

Grooming is an extremely important part of an animal's daily repertoire. Using front paws, saliva, tongue, teeth and hind nails, rabbits spend a substantial part of their day in this activity. They nibble away at bits of vegetation caught in their fur, they wash away water and splashes of mud and rub and scratch to comb their hair, so to speak. The rabbit's fur coat is its protection against the cold, the wet and sunburn. A rabbit needs to maintain its coat in good condition; otherwise it may quickly succumb to hypothermia or infestation by mites, or suffer from fly strike (see Maggots, p. 150).

Rabbits also use grooming as a means of strengthening relationships, an affiliative behaviour. They will gently lick and nibble each other's fur, especially on those difficult-to-get-at bits like the backs of ears and between the shoulders. If your rabbit decides to lick your hand you are honoured and should react appropriately. It is, after all, the nearest your rabbit can get to giving you an affectionate stroke.

All rabbits benefit from a weekly grooming session with a rubber brush such as the Zoom Groom designed for cats. Longer-coated breeds, the Angoras and Cashmeres, will need brushing daily if they are to be kept free of tangles. Tangles should be cut along the line of growth and then gently teased apart from the tip of the hair back towards the body. Use a comb with rotating teeth, such as the appropriately named Untangler available from pet shops. If you are not too fussy about looks, then just snip the tangles off. Please groom your rabbit more often in hot weather.

Rabbits have quite thin, very sensitive skin. You need to be careful and gentle when grooming your pet, as a single painful experience may well set the stage for aggression in the future (see Fear aggression, p. 125, and Learnt aggression, p. 148). If you use too much pressure, you may hurt the rabbit's back or tummy; remember just how much bigger and stronger you are. This is even worse if you use a hard metal brush or comb. If you do not believe me, try it on your own head. Do not pull or yank at tangles; this can be extremely painful, as anyone with long hair knows. It is useful to start grooming your rabbit when it is a kitten, so it can get used to the procedure. You can, of course, make it even more pleasurable by making it a time when your rabbit has access to some favourite nibbles. You can brush while your rabbit munches happily.

Growling

A growling rabbit is not inviting company (see Grunting, below). Unheeded growling is usually swiftly followed by the gnashing of a sharp set of teeth. It does not take many repeat performances for you to take notice of the growls emitted by your rabbit. Consider the body language the rabbit displays when growling. Are his ears flat or upright? Is he leaning towards you or away? Is he in pain or frightened, or being bossy and territorial? Is he actually growling at you or at the dog he can see approaching from behind you?

Grunting

To the unpractised ear a rabbit which is grunting may sound rather like one which is growling. Indeed, a grunt may be the prelude to a growl if the individual to whom it is directed does not take the hint and move away. As with our own language, the meaning of the vocal message is often clarified by the body language accompanying it. This is why we have more misunderstandings when we talk to people on the telephone; we cannot see their face and body and so miss out on a whole aspect of the message they are sending. This problem of only 'hearing' part of the message is why we often misinterpret the behaviour of other animals. For example, a dog can bark when it is aggressive, playful, alert, fearful and in greeting; the bark alone will not tell you the motivation of the dog.

What she is actually doing is flirting.

Rabbits are less complicated but the principle is the same. To try and understand your rabbit you need to consider its body language, the situation and any sounds it may be making. For example, you may be surprised to see your female rabbit performing what appears to be a Red Indian war dance. She will run in circles around your feet, making grunting noises. What she is actually doing is flirting. This behaviour can happen whether the doe is kept alone or with another rabbit. It is triggered by her hormones and indicates that she is prepared to indulge in some courtship and mating.

H

Head shaking

Question

My rabbit tends to hold his head on one side which gives him quite an endearing, quizzical look. He also has bouts of shaking his head, as if in disbelief at what I have just said to him. Can you please explain his behaviour? In case you need to know, he is a Miniature Lop and is one year old.

Answer

While I can imagine that a rabbit with its head cocked on one side might look endearing, it is in fact a sign that all is not well. Rabbits of all types can suffer from ear infections. The most usual cause is canker, which is the result of microscopic organisms called mites. An early symptom of this is rapid head shaking as your rabbit tries to clear his ear out. If it is not treated, more permanent damage can occur to the inside of the ear. This may be why your rabbit now appears to be a lop-sided Lop. I suggest a trip to the vet is called for.

Ear problems can happen in rabbits with long or short, lop or pricked ears. Lop-eared animals do seem to be somewhat more prone to problems, probably because the ear cannot drain so well and also because the shape of the ear keeps the inside warm and cosy for those mites to live and breed in happily. Make an ear examination a part of your regular weekly rabbit health check. A healthy ear should look clean inside and smell sweet. Do do the smell check, as you can often smell an infected ear before the infection has reached the outer ear and become visible. Do not attempt to clean out your pet's ear with cotton buds or similar; you may do more harm than good. If the ear is dirty, get it checked by the vet.

Homeopathy

Homeopathy is an ancient form of medicine which has recently been taken up by members of the veterinary profession. Some owners prefer this veterinary discipline of alternative medicine to conventional medicine. If you are interested in finding such a veterinary surgeon in your area then any local surgery should be able to point you in the right direction. Some homeopathic veterinarians will also take referrals from your own vet.

House training

House training is an important part of ensuring that you and your rabbit can live peacefully together indoors. Forever cleaning up after your rabbit is not going to enhance your relationship. As rabbits use latrines in the wild, you can harness this aspect of their behaviour to train your rabbit to toilet where you wish, in a litter tray.

When you first bring your future house rabbit indoors, have ready an indoor pen which is big enough to contain a litter tray, a food bowl, a hay rack, a water bottle and enough space for your rabbit to move around. This should be placed in a quiet corner of the room where the rabbit can see and hear you. Line the cage with a newspaper and cover it with straw. Put some shredded paper in the litter tray. Place a few of your rabbit's droppings or some urine-soaked paper from its travelling basket into the tray. You are now ready for your rabbit.

If you place the hay rack so the rabbit has to be in the

If you have a dog it may learn to follow your rabbit just in case . . .

tray in order to nibble, you will find it easier to train the rabbit to the litter tray. It is advisable to leave the rabbit in the pen for a couple of days so it can make it truly its own safe place. This will involve it leaving some pellets around its cage as a way of scent-marking it. The cage should always be a safe place for your rabbit that it will want to return to, to sleep and toilet. Always coax your rabbit out of its kennel, never force it. In order to keep the tray recognised as the place to toilet, replace a small bit of used litter when you clean it out.

Your rabbit may have the odd accident when it is out and about in the house. These will be hard pellets and can easily be picked or hoovered up. If you have a dog, it may learn to follow your rabbit just in case it deposits any droppings. Most dogs seem to think they are excellent treats and you need not worry as they will do no harm.

I

Indoor rabbits

Question
I have recently heard that rabbits can be kept in the house. Is this beneficial for them, considering they are outdoor creatures? What are the advantages and disadvantages of keeping a rabbit in the house? Can only young animals be introduced to this way of life, or could I being my five-year-old New Zealand White, Bounce, in from the cold?

Answer
The keeping of rabbits as indoor pets is not a new phenomenon but one which has become ever more popular. Although they are still in the minority, many rabbit owners are realising they can develop a deeper and more rewarding relationship with a rabbit kept indoors. One reason for this is that we tend to spend more time with our pets if they are in the warmth of the living room than if we keep them in the garden, particularly given the tendency of the British weather to be wet!

The rabbits themselves also benefit from a more interesting environment, greater opportunity for exercise and the additional company of people, of particular relevance where there is only one rabbit. It is, though, important to remember they are still rabbits; they need to be given a suitable diet and might not approve of everything we humans do. Rabbits do not like loud or sudden noise, but can be quite partial to music and will sit by your feet as you play the piano. They are better kept in a smoke-free environment as they can be susceptible to respiratory problems. In addition you need to realise that rabbit habits mean they cannot fit into a human home without some preparation on your part: homes need rabbit proofing (see Chewing, p. 109, and Pica, p. 166).

There are many ways of ensuring a rabbit does not do too much damage. Block off areas to which you do not wish your rabbit to have access. Provide your rabbit with a safe place where you can leave it when you are not there to supervise; a puppy pen or indoor kennel is ideal. Cover any exposed wires. Your local DIY store is likely to have plastic ducting you can place over any electric or telephone cables, or even over skirting board. These can be painted to match your decor.

Never leave your rabbit out and about unsupervised, as they can get up to all sorts of mischief. And if that involves chewing cables it may be very expensive mischief indeed.

You ask whether Bounce is too old to become a house rabbit. The answer is no, but a qualified no. If Bounce is of a nervous disposition and has not had much opportunity to learn about the world outside his hutch, then you need to introduce him to this new way of life gradually. He will not be used to the strange smells and sounds of your home and may even be somewhat agoraphobic. Some of the suggestions I made in the sections on agoraphobia (p. 90) and babies (p. 103) could be adapted to getting Bounce prepared for his new environment.

For more information about the keeping of house rabbits, contact the British Houserabbit Association or, in the United States, the Houserabbit Society.

Injections

Your rabbit will need to be vaccinated against Myxomatosis and VHD (see pp. 154 and 188). It may also need to have an injection of antibiotics in order to combat a serious case of ear canker, for instance. The veterinary surgeon will use the loose skin around the scruff of the neck as an injection site. Rabbits tolerate this very well so there is no need to worry. You may, of course, wish to make the trip to the vet as pleasant as possible for your rabbit. To do so, take with you some of his or her favourite titbits and offer them before and during the injection.

Introductions

The easiest way of introducing rabbits is to buy a pair of litter brothers or brother and sister. That way they have been introduced from birth. Rabbits who are introduced at a very young age, before 12 weeks, will also usually settle down quite easily.

Introducing rabbits at a later stage is more difficult, though it can be fairly easily accomplished if one is a neutered male and the other female. It needs to be done gradually and the process overseen so that any squabbles that start can be stopped quickly. Place the rabbits in a large open space (fenced in of course) which is new to both rabbits, so it is the territory of neither rabbit. A room in the house could be used for the purpose. Break up the space with objects such as boxes and buckets which allow the animals to get out of each other's sight. Scatter around plenty of delicious greens, crackers, even fruit, so the rabbits can make pleasant associations with each other. There is likely to be some initial chasing and perhaps a bit of scuffling. Assuming all goes well, separate them for the night in their home hutches and repeat the procedure every day for a week or so or until you see them lying relaxed next to each other. Then introduce them to their joint hutch and pen (a different one) for a few minutes, increasing it to a few hours and then overnight.

A similar procedure can be used when introducing rabbits to cavies. But please ensure that the cavy has sufficient hiding places which are inaccessible to the rabbit, such as boxes with a cavy-sized hole cut into them or some clay piping.

You may have to re-introduce animals which have been separated for some reason, such as a trip to the vet's. This can be made easier if you put some bedding from the home cage into the animal's travelling box. You could also rub the returning rabbit with some of the bedding to give it the 'colony' scent and mask the odours it will have picked up on its travels. Do supervise re-introductions and make sure plenty of goodies are scattered around so that the proceedings go as peaceably as possible.

J

Jumping

Rabbits can jump, though they are not as well designed for this as other mammals. Their bodies are designed for hopping movements, rather than running and jumping. When running from predators, rabbits will often jump in mid-stride, twisting their bodies as they go. This helps them change direction at speed. If you are planning to teach your rabbit some agility and provide it with jumps, make sure these are not too high and that your rabbit has had the opportunity to exercise when young, and thus does not have weak muscles and bones (see Agility, p. 88, and Excitement, p. 123).

Rabbits are quite expert at escaping and can combine the arts of jumping and climbing to get themselves over barriers such as wire fences, so it is sensible to make sure your rabbit's run has a securely fixed top. There is a report of a Dwarf Lop who managed to scale a 1.5 metre (4 ft)-high stable door. I do not know if she holds the world record.

Juvenile behaviour

Rabbits reach sexual maturity when they are about four months old, but they are not yet behaviourally adult or fully grown. Just like human teenagers and young adult dogs, some young adult rabbits go through a rather 'bolshie' stage. This is the time when they would normally be

finding their place among the adults of the group and
you may find your youngster gets rather mischievous and
even a little nippy.

If, for instance, he or she nips you to move you out of
the way, perhaps when you are sharing the sofa, say a firm
'No', pick your rabbit up and put it on the floor. It will
soon learn that you will not be intimidated in this way.

K

Kittening

Question

I have a lovely Dutch doe called Evita. She is very tame and gentle and I would love to breed from her. I have found the man of her dreams, well, that is what I think he is, another Dutch called Bugs. Please could you tell me how I should go about this 'arranged marriage'?

Answer

My first concern is that you have thought this through very carefully. Rabbit kittens are, in my view, absolutely adorable, and judging by the numbers sold in pet shops

How should I go about this arranged marriage?

I am not alone in this attitude. However, kittens grow up and people all too frequently get bored with the resultant adult rabbit. Please remember that over 24,000 ended up in rescue in 1997. This figure does not include all those rabbits which were passed on to friends and neighbours or put to sleep because they were no longer wanted. In addition, breeders of fancy rabbits do not keep all the offspring they produce and culling the excess is a common practice. Basically, far more domestic rabbits are bred every year than there are homes available. So my question is: can you be sure you will be able to find good, permanent homes for the youngsters you are planning to bring into existence? Will you take them back, at any time in their life, if they can no longer be kept by their owners?

Assuming you have decided that you will be a responsible breeder, a lot of good advice about rabbit breeding is available and you may wish to contact the British Rabbit Council or the American Rabbit Breeders Association for information about Dutch rabbit breeders in your area. You do not say how old Evita is, but she should be at least six months old before you put her to a male. If she is three or four years old, it may be rather late to start. Either way, it is a good idea to have her checked over by the vet to make sure she is fit and healthy. Do check her teeth are not maloccluded as this may be an inherited condition. If they are, then no matter how sweet her nature, I strongly urge you to abandon the idea of breeding from her. Do also have Bugs's teeth checked for the same reason.

Does do not take overly kindly to males being put into their cage. Evita may well give Bugs a telling off which would put him off the whole idea. It is better to take Evita to Bugs's hutch and run complex. Make sure they have plenty of room and lots of nibbles around. This will allow them to get used to each other and indulge in some courtship. If she is obviously uninterested, and possibly even quite grumpy from his attentions, then she is not ready to mate. Remove her and try her again later, the next day.

Commercial or fancy breeders will often put the rabbits in a small cage for mating, but I am assuming you would like her to have as natural a mating as possible.

From the above statements it is obvious that you will need to supervise the proceedings. Mating itself is very quick. The male straddles the doe, gripping her neck and making some rapid pelvic thrusts. Once he has ejaculated the buck will fall off the doe. It may be accompanied by a short scream from either of the pair; this is quite normal, so do not worry. If Bugs is inexperienced, he may have a few abortive attempts at mating, possibly even trying the wrong end of Evita. Again do not worry, she will soon put him right. Once you have had a successful mating, you may wish to try again the next day, just to make sure she has been impregnated, but this is not essential.

Approximately 30 days later, Evita will give birth. During her pregnancy, make sure she has plenty of good-quality hay and some rabbit mix to eat and fresh water to drink. If she has access to her run for exercise and, hopefully sunshine, then all should proceed well. About a week before she is due, provide her with a nest box, which should have sides about 10 cm (4 in) high to contain the kittens. Make sure she has plenty of straw and hay to make her nest with. The box should be placed in a dark corner of her hutch; her bedroom area is fine. As her time approaches, Evita may get more aggressive towards you. This, too, is normal behaviour. You will also notice that she starts to pluck fur from her body to line her nest.

When you think she has given birth, do leave well alone for 24 hours. Then, blocking off her access to the nest box for a few minutes, carefully check the nest for any dead babies and remove them. Do not handle the babies unnecessarily. If you do Evita may become very upset and either desert her young or cannibalise them. Before letting her back in with the young, if possible give her a quick stroke.

Do not bother to clean the hutch thoroughly for a week,

other than to remove Evita's droppings from her toilet site (see Maggots, p. 150). Let Evita get on with being a mother with as little interference as possible. Again try not to handle the kittens too much and, if you do, then also stroke Evita so she has your scent on her as well.

After about 18 days the kittens should be exploring their world and can be handled quite freely, though they should not be taken away from their home cage for more than a few minutes at a time. Between three and four weeks, Evita may start to wean them off her milk. It is helpful if they can remain with her for another fortnight or three weeks before they go to their new homes. But do prepare them for this. See the suggestions made under the section Babies (p. 103). Throughout this period, ensure the rabbits have plenty of good-quality hay to eat.

As my own research has shown, given a suitable environment with plenty of room and places for privacy, bucks can be kept successfully with a doe and her young. Perhaps this should not surprise us, as it happens all the time in the wild. However, I do not recommend it as a standard practice. The doe will be mated again soon after having given birth and, until separated, will be producing offspring repeatedly. Pregnancy and lactation take a lot of energy out of a doe and repeated pregnancies will inevitably shorten her life. In the commercial world, where repeated matings are common, a doe is usually 'discarded' after a year. In the fancy world a doe is rarely bred after three years of age if she has had a number of litters.

As a final note on this subject, I will once again ask you to think carefully before deciding to breed your pet rabbit. You are responsible not only for her life but, ultimately, for those of all her offspring.

L

Learnt aggression

Rabbits are more than capable of learning that aggression can get them what they want, which is basically the removal of whatever it is they find frightening or painful. We have already seen that this was a contributing factor in Sloppy's aggression to his young owner Sam (see Fear aggression, p. 125).

Question

I own two Flemish Giant rabbits, Branston and Pickle. They are litter brothers, both neutered, and live happily together. I got both rabbits at the same time, when they were seven weeks old, but they could not be more different in temperament. Branston has always been more twitchy or nervous than Pickle. I am seriously considering changing their names to Chalk and Cheese. Every day I or my husband carry both rabbits to a large run in the garden where they nibble the grass, sit on or in the clay pipes in the run and have long conversations through the wire with my Newfoundland dog. I have no problems with either rabbit in the hutch, and no problems at all with Pickle. But Branston is another kettle of fish, or armful of rabbit.

When I open the hutch door, Branston will approach us with his ears forward and nuzzle an offered hand. He will remain relaxed while his head is scratched. However, any movement of a hand towards his back causes him to flatten his ears and move away. If you continue, which we have to in order to get him out to the run, he growls and runs around the hutch, occasionally showing some aggression to Pickle. When he is finally caught, Branston will remain quite still for a few seconds and then bite and kick. I have to say this usually means a mad dash to the run to get him put down on the ground. As you can imagine, several kilos of rabbit (Branston weighs 11 kg (24 lb)), sinking its teeth into your arm or kicking violently is no fun. My husband and I both have scars on our arms and on one occasion Branston's efforts required a trip to the hospital and stitches. Help! We have had two years of this and cannot take much more.

Answer
The behaviour you describe indicates Branston is very fearful of being lifted, but not of human hands *per se*. It is likely that at some point he has suffered some trauma such as being dropped or squeezed too hard, possibly before you bought him at seven weeks, as suggested by his early nervous demeanour. A single incident is sufficient for such a behaviour to develop. Negative associations can be learnt with a single exposure to an aversive stimulus and pain is very aversive.

Branston has learnt that aggression works and he gets what he wants, namely to be put on the ground. I suggest that you redesign the cage and hutch so that they are an integral unit, thereby negating the need to lift the rabbits every day. Then follow the procedure outlined for Sloppy (see Fear aggression, p. 125).

M

Maggots

Also known as fly strike, an infestation of maggots can quickly debilitate and kill a rabbit. A single fly can be the cause of the problem, but where there is one fly there are usually several. A fly wishing to lay her eggs will be attracted to places which are warm, moist and smelly. Odours, particularly those of decaying matter or faeces, indicate there will be a food supply for her developing young. Small, badly ventilated rabbit hutches with little free-moving air are perfect. If the rabbit itself has faeces or urine stuck to its coat, the fly will be attracted to that area, the rabbit being the warmest thing in the hutch. The fly will lay her eggs on the dirty coat, usually near the rabbit's anus. In warm weather the eggs may take only eight hours to hatch into the ravenously hungry larvae we call maggots.

The maggots will quickly eat the faeces stuck to your rabbit's coat, but this is unlikely to satisfy them. They will then proceed to devour your rabbit alive, literally. If the rabbit has an open sore, this will be an obvious place to start, but the maggots will also work their way to the soft tissues lining the anal passage and chew their way through them. The damage can be horrific. To help them digest this raw, living meat, the maggots produce chemicals which are toxic to the rabbit, making it enter a state of shock. The rabbit may never recover. If it is to have a chance swift action needs to be taken. Get the rabbit to the vet, now.

Fly strike is a dreadful condition and not one that any reasonable person would wish on a living creature. For the pet owner whose rabbit suffers this condition, and maybe dies from it, there can be intense feelings of shock and guilt. But fly strike can be avoided, and without too much difficulty on the part of the owner.

First consider your rabbit's environment. Many traditional rabbit hutches provide the perfect conditions— perfect for the fly that is. They have a wire mesh door on one side of the front, but no ventilation holes at the back to draw the air through. Obviously you do not wish your rabbit to be exposed to draughts, but drilling a series of holes a couple of centimetres (one inch) in diameter three-quarters of the way up the back wall will protect your rabbit from draught but allow the air to circulate. This will help prevent fly strike and respiratory problems as well.

The second consideration is the size of your rabbit's home. Is it really big enough? As you may have gathered by now, I think the rabbit should have an integrated hutch and run system so that it can choose to sit in or out. (See Predation, p. 167.) If this is not feasible in your case, does your rabbit at least have sufficient room in the hutch to sit well away from her toilet area and from any damp bedding? You may think that if you carry your rabbit from her hutch to a run every day then she will be okay, but if the hutch is small and she is near damp and dirty bedding at night she may still get fly strike. Flies can strike late in the evening and early in the morning, before you are ready to move your rabbit.

Is the hutch clean? Soiled bedding and damp newspaper should be removed every day, and the hutch given a proper clean-out once a week. A good scrub with a mild solution of washing-up liquid or commercial cage cleaner will do the trick. A good old-fashioned scrubbing brush is essential, especially if you have a wooden cage, and you will need elbow grease to clean all the nooks and crannies. Ensure the hutch is completely dry before you reline it with newspaper (a thick layer) and her fresh bedding. Do not use an insecticide in or near your rabbit's home, as it could be just as harmful as the fly strike you are trying to prevent.

Make it part of your daily routine when you feed your rabbit to check her rear end for any dirt, faeces stuck to her fur or diarrhoea. Clean off any you see using warm water to soften it, or ask your veterinary surgeon for a proprietary cleaner. Remember your rabbit could get a bout of diarrhoea if it has a sudden change in diet.

Many rabbits who suffer fly strike are very well cared for, in fact usually too much so. A fat rabbit may seem to be healthy, but it is a case of potentially killing your rabbit by too much kindness. An obese rabbit may not be able to reach its anus easily and so cannot catch the soft faecal pellets it produces (see Diet, pp. 35 and 113). These are likely to become stuck to its fur and cause matting. They are very attractive to flies. A fat rabbit is also unable to clean itself properly.

An inappropriate diet can also mean the rabbit is likely to suffer from maloccluded teeth. This in turn may mean the rabbit is unable to groom itself adequately. A potential for fly strike is just one of the many problems which can result from a rabbit having poor teeth (see Diet, p. 113).

So, if you keep your rabbit clean, give it plenty of room and feed it properly and therefore well, you should never have the distress of seeing your pet suffer from the horrors of fly strike.

Marking

Rabbits mark their environment in order to claim it for themselves (see Scent-marking, p. 74). They do this by leaving their scent on prominent objects and on members of their colony, which of course can include their owners.

Both male and female rabbits will use latrine sites . . .

The most commonly used form of marking is when the rabbit 'chins' the object. He or she will gently rub its chin on the site to be marked and, in so doing, leave a trace of secretion from its scent gland. This is obviously attractive to rabbits, and presumably quite smelly, but it is not noticed by humans. Nor does it seem to do any harm to furniture and furnishings. If you put a new object in your rabbit's territory, whether in its run or your living room, then it will be investigated and well chinned.

Both male and female rabbits will use latrine sites for fouling. These also act as territorial markers. Occasional droppings will also be deposited away from the latrine site. Unlike male dogs which seem to have to spray every lamp-post with urine, rabbits do not tend to spray objects. Spraying of other rabbits, or people, is usually related to courtship (see Enurination, p. 121), though a jet of urine can also be aimed at a subordinate. Neutering can help reduce this behaviour.

Maternal aggression
Maternal aggression is so called because it refers to aggression which is only displayed when a female is in late pregnancy or has babies. Maternal aggression is common in animals and is based in the mother's instinctive desire to protect her young. This desire is very strong; after all, reproduction is the main reason for life. Consequently, female rabbits can be extremely aggressive in order to acquire or protect the resources they require for their

young. Does sometimes fight to the death over the right of access to a good spot in which to dig a nest burrow. So, if your doe is having a bout of maternal aggression, beware. Remember that, as Kipling noted, there is nothing more deadly than the female of the species.

Maternal aggression can also occur when a female has a pseudo-pregnancy. This can be triggered even in an unneutered doe who lives with a neutered buck. In this situation the female's hormones are telling her that she is ready to be mated (see Breeding, p. 46) and she may flirt with and even be mounted by the male. Obviously as he is castrated he cannot inseminate her, but the act of being mounted may be sufficient to cause her to ovulate and so become pseudo-pregnant.

If your doe is becoming aggressive when you go near her hutch, pen or indoor kennel, it may be that she is showing maternal aggression. Try to remember when her aggression started. Did it start in early spring? Does it switch on for a period of two or three weeks and then, just as suddenly, she seems to return to her normal relaxed self? If so, then her aggression is likely to be hormonal and the answer is to have her neutered (see Neutering, p. 159).

Myxomatosis
The Myxomatosis virus was introduced to the rabbit population in Britain in 1953 as a means of controlling the increasing numbers of wild rabbits that were regarded as pests in the developing agricultural economy. The virus was taken from populations of cottontail rabbits in Central and South America, where the animals have developed a natural immunity to the infection, which produces in them only a small lump on their skin and mild sneezing. Because European rabbits had no resistance to the virus, the consequences of their coming into contact with it were much more serious. When it was introduced, Myxomatosis killed 99.99 per cent of British wild rabbits. Since then

the wild population has developed a degree of immunity and has recovered its numbers leading to more recent control measures (see Quantity, p. 71).

The virus is passed between rabbits either by direct contact, or through transmission by mosquitoes, biting flies and particularly rabbit fleas. The virus passes into the bloodstream and, if susceptible, the rabbit shows signs of infection within a week. The first is conjunctivitis, where the rabbit's eyes become swollen and inflamed, with a sticky discharge. Next, a discharge also appears from the nose, and the rabbit may sneeze and have difficulty breathing. Lumps appear on the area around the eyes, on the ears and nose and also around the animal's back end. Infected rabbits usually die within one or two weeks of the first signs appearing, although obviously it is kinder to put them to sleep before the symptoms become too severe.

Infection by Myxomatosis can easily be prevented by regular vaccination. This usually requires a yearly booster, although in some high-risk areas, more frequent vaccination is recommended for your pet's full protection.

Nails

Question

I have a delightful house rabbit called Oz who is two years old. I obtained Oz when he was ten months old from a neighbour who had to move to a new job location and was unable to take him with her. He gives us great pleasure and is an entertaining companion who is into everything, but he has one major fault—his feet. Or, to be more exact, his claws. I have never had a rabbit before, but have had cats. I am used to cats withdrawing their claws and realise that Oz is unable to do this, or does not think it appropriate. But they are so long they are like talons. Indeed in this respect he is becoming more and more like a wizard. Can you help?

Answer

It all sounds rather painful, both for you and Oz. Unlike cats, rabbits do not have retractable claws, but nails which, like our own or a dog's, are permanently exposed. Your cat presumably had a scratching post or used some handy tree in the garden to keep its claws neat, short and sharp. Rabbits would naturally wear down their nails through digging. When they are unable to do so, whether kept indoors or out, then it is our responsibility to ensure that their nails do not grow too long. If they are too long they will cause pain to the rabbit as they push the toes out of alignment. It is necessary to clip your rabbit's nails regularly to just before the quick, so that they do not bleed. This is easily done, using a set of small dog nail clippers. If you do not wish to do this yourself then ask your veterinarian to do it for you, or at least show you how it should be done. Rabbit nails grow more quickly in young animals and in those which are more sedentary. Growth rate will also be influenced by diet; if fed on grass, they will grow more quickly in the spring and summer when the grass is more nutritious. Rabbits have five toes on the front feet and four on the back, so make sure you trim all eighteen. Then you and Oz can both enjoy cuddles in comfort.

Neck biting

Question
I would like to have a guinea-pig to live with my rabbit, a male Californian called Brutus, so named because of his size rather than his temperament. He really is a gentle giant. However, I am rather worried because I have been told by some people that this would be fine and by others that he will kill any guinea-pig I introduce. Could you please clarify this for me?

Answer
There are many people who do not believe that rabbits and cavies (guinea-pigs) can be kept together. This stems from the fact that sometimes a cavy will be killed by the rabbit. Assuming the two have been introduced successfully and have lived together amicably, it can still happen that the rabbit will kill the cavy by biting its neck. This problem is usually seen when the rabbit is male. During the breeding season, it is possible that the male will turn its amorous attentions to the cavy. If the cavy has nowhere to retreat to, then the rabbit may well attempt to mate the poor beast.

During the act of mating the male tends to grip the female by the neck for support (see Kittening, p. 144). If he does this to a much smaller animal, such as a cavy, and begins to thrust with his pelvis, then he is likely to do some damage, or the cavy may die of shock. From the cavy's point of view it must feel like being attacked by a predator.

If you are going to get a guinea-pig to keep Brutus company, then it is very important that they have plenty of room and the guinea-pig has places to retreat from Brutus's advances (see Introductions, p. 140). This is true when housing any two animals together, but has particular significance given the disparity in size between a Californian, which can weight over four kilos (nearly nine pounds), and a cavy. It is also worth considering having Brutus neutered to deter any sexual urges he may have. My first two rabbits, Thumper and Nomad, were both male and had cavies as companions. Though neither was neutered, (it was not common practice 30 years ago) they did have large hutch/run complexes. I never had an early death, the cavies living for at least five years and the rabbits for substantially longer.

Nervousness
Every rabbit is an individual, and its adult behaviour is determined in part by characteristics it has inherited from its parents and in part by its experiences. How an animal reacts to a given stimulus, such as a noise, will be influenced by its inherited personality traits. Of course rabbits are all reactive to stimuli indicating potential danger, but some will be more reactive than others. There is evidence from many species, in particular from research on dogs, that nervousness is an inherited trait.

The heritability of nervousness is just as true for rabbits. While there will be individual differences within a litter, let alone across breeds, some generalisations can be made. Smaller breeds tend to be more nervous than the larger breeds—another good reason for having a large breed if your rabbit is to live in a noisy household or if there are children around. Kittens whose mother or father is nervous are likely to be more nervous than those whose parents are more relaxed, so it is important to see both parents, if possible, when choosing a pet rabbit. Responsible breeders will have done their best to make sure your future pet is well socialised (see Babies, p. 103). It is to be hoped that they also will have bred their kittens from easy-going parents, but you should be aware that some breeders are more interested in how their rabbits look than their temperament. This problem is also true in the dog world, if the breeder is concerned with an animal's potential to win shows rather than to be a good pet.

Neutering

Question
I have been advised to have my two male rabbits neutered. I am not convinced that this is a good idea as I have heard that neutering an animal will change its character and make it prone to obesity. Please could you explain to me the advantages and disadvantages of neutering?

Answer
Neutering an animal means that it is de-sexed. When done to males it is called castration and with females, spaying. It is accomplished by removing the sexual organs. In the male this is a simple and quick procedure where the testes are removed from the scrotal sac. For the female, it is rather more complicated and requires the removal of both the ovaries and the uterus.

Whether your animal is male or female, neutering will mean a stay in the veterinary hospital. The rabbit will be anaesthetised for a short period while the operation takes place. In the last few years there have been great advances in surgical techniques applied to rabbits and the operation

Any pet rabbit can become overweight if it is fed too much.

should go smoothly. In the past it was common to castrate males without anaesthesia by making them immobile (see Trancing, p. 179). Given that the rabbit is conscious in this state, and likely to feel pain, this is not a method I would advocate. Anaesthetising rabbits is now a common procedure and would be the preferred option. As rabbits are not as amenable to anaesthesia as some other species, and not all veterinary surgeons have had much experience of operating on rabbits, you may wish to discuss neutering further with your vet, and possibly ask to be referred to one who specialises in rabbits.

You ask whether neutering will give your rabbits a tendency to put on weight. Neutering can reduce an animal's level of activity slightly in that the rabbit will be less territorial. However, any pet rabbit can become overweight if it is fed too much. You need to check the weight of your rabbits on a weekly basis and adjust their feed accordingly.

As for a change in character, neutering in itself does not change an animal's character, though it does reduce or eliminate the drive to perform certain behaviours which are hormonal in basis. These include sexual behaviour, territoriality and, for does, maternal aggression. If your bucks are to be kept together they are less likely to fight if they are castrated.

There are some other positive physical benefits to neutering. Your buck rabbits will not be prone to testicular cancer and neutered does will not get cancer of the ovaries or uterus.

All in all, I would suggest that the advantages of neutering for all pet rabbits outweigh any disadvantages.

O

Old age

Rabbits can live for a decade or more, though this does vary slightly with breed. Obviously, if your rabbit is to have a long life it needs to be fed an appropriate diet and kept in a clean, spacious and stimulating environment. One rabbit, called Flopsy, who made it into the record books, lived to the ripe old age of 18 years and 10 months.

As rabbits get older they are likely to suffer from complaints similar to ours. Their hearing and eyesight may deteriorate, making them a bit more reactive when you pick them up, so it is advisable to talk to them so they know you are there and do not get too much of a surprise. Likewise, older rabbits may become rather cantankerous because they are in some pain. Their joints are likely to be a bit stiff and they may even have some arthritis. Do handle them gently.

However long your rabbit lives, whether for two years or ten, it is totally dependent on you for the quality of its life. Your pet will have a better life, and you will get far more pleasure from it, if you take on this responsibility fully. As you have read this far, I am sure that is what you want to do anyway.

P, Q

Pain-associated aggression
Rabbits, like us, can become exceedingly grumpy if they
are feeling under the weather or are in pain. Pain may
be temporary and easily treated, such as a mild case of
ear mites, or its source may be more subtle and chronic.
Arthritis, bone deformities or strain from not being given
enough room to develop properly, or teeth problems
resulting in spurs entering the soft tissues of the face,
abscesses or merely a lacerated tongue can all make your
rabbit aggressive. If your once friendly rabbit starts to
behave aggressively, your first port of call should be your
veterinary surgeon to make sure there is no medical
reason for the change in behaviour.

Phobias
Phobias are defined as fears which are irrational. We sometimes consider that animals have phobias. Certainly animals can appear to be excessively fearful of certain stimuli,
even though we try to reassure them, for example the dog
who buries its head under your bed in a thunderstorm and
shakes terribly. Much as we stroke and comfort them, they
only seem to get worse. This is often exactly what happens
because, from the dog's viewpoint, shaking is apparently
the correct behaviour. After all, his owners are patting him
and that is what they do when he does the right thing. Dogs
are social animals and will learn to some extent by watching

others around them. One way of preventing a dog becoming scared of thunder is to bring out its favourite toy or food. Helping a dog overcome an already established fear is more complicated. For further information, see John Fisher's *Why Does My Dog . . . ?*

Rabbits, too, can appear to suffer from irrational fears. Whether they are truly irrational is debatable. There are those who will argue that at some point the fear was reinforced and therefore, at that time, the fear would have been rational, though it may no longer be an appropriate fear. That is different from being irrational. I personally agree with this view. The power of learning by association is quite amazing, particularly when it relates to fearful consequences associated with a stimulus or an event. It is important for any animal to learn and remember lessons about things which are potentially dangerous, lessons that need to be remembered for life. I would contend that what we class as phobias in animals (and probably also in people) are really fears which are inappropriate and for which we do not know the original, appropriate, association the animal made.

Question

I have a house rabbit, of no particular breed, called Velvet. He is very sweet and I have no problems with him, other than the normal occasional nibble at something he shouldn't. One of his behaviours does puzzle me, though. He appears to have a phobia about the pedal bin in the kitchen. While he is happy to come into the kitchen with me, he will not venture to the side cavity where the bin is kept. Instead, he gives it a wide berth in order to get from one end of the kitchen to the other. I do not think it is the noise of the bin which worries him as he does not run away if I put anything in it. What is even odder is that he used to like sitting near it under the work surface. Could you please explain this, and is there anything we can do to help him?

Answer

I can understand why you think Velvet's fear is irrational; after all, what has the bin ever done to him? It certainly is an inappropriate fear, in that the bin is really a harmless object. However, it may not be irrational in that Velvet has made an association with the bin and something unpleasant occurring. As you have not been able to give a clue to what this may have been, it is possible that it happened when you were not there or seemed so insignificant at the time that it did not register. But what may be insignificant to us may be very salient, important, to Velvet. For example, he may have been sitting there quietly minding his own business when someone put something in the bin and missed; this could have been liquid or solid, but it startled him sufficiently for him to decide that this was no longer a safe place. Another possibility is that he was in this safe place when he was ferreted out of it by an enthusiastic child or inquisitive dog or cat. You may be able to think of some instance which explains his behaviour, but often we do not know what the initial stimulus was which indicated to the animal that there was something to be feared.

You ask if you can do anything to help Velvet overcome his fear. You can, but it will take time and patience. I would suggest that first you move the pedal bin from the kitchen altogether (perhaps into the garage for a few days). This will clarify whether it is the bin itself or the location which is the trouble. Having moved the bin, lay a trail of Velvet's favourite titbits from a safe area of the kitchen to the space where the pedal bin was. As the trail gets nearer to the pedal bin space, increase the quantity and quality of titbits—quality, that is, from Velvet's point of view, namely the most tasty treats, should be nearest to the space. If he is happy to enter the space, then the cue for his fear is the bin itself. If he is not happy to enter the space then this fear must be vanquished before you proceed to re-introduce the bin.

The principle is the same in both cases, namely giving him the opportunity to associate the space and bin with good things. This will include food as described, but you could also sit down by or even in the space and encourage him to be with you. If the bin is the problem, you will need to put it in other areas of the house, so he can make positive associations with it away from the kitchen before you place it back in the kitchen, finally working on the combined stimulus of bin and kitchen.

Pica

This is usually a problem reported by owners of indoor rabbits and refers to the rabbit's habit of seemingly incessant chewing—of electric cables, plastic bottles, prized books (especially if bound in leather) and treasured furniture. Often the problem is solved by banning the animal to an outside cage or rehoming it.

Unlike pica in cats and dogs, the ingestion of inappropriate material such as plastic or electric cables by the rabbit is not commonly a symptom of a deeper psychological problem, but reflects its anatomy. Rabbits have open-rooted teeth which require constant wear, combined with a strong drive to forage. Dangling wires are particularly irresistible to rabbits. This may have something to do with burrowing behaviour, where rabbits have to chew through plant and tree roots which cross their burrows. The only solution is for owners to rabbit-proof their home: limit access to cables, etc., use 'No' and taste deterrents where applicable (see Chewing, p. 109, and Indoor rabbits, p. 138), provide the rabbit with suitable objects to 'slice and grind' in the form of appropriate foodstuffs to satisfy the need to forage, and lots of toys. Finally, and most importantly, do not leave your rabbit loose in your house when unattended.

Question

My daughter's rabbit, Willow, lives in a hutch and run in the garden but often comes indoors in the evening for a few hours. My daughter takes her up to her bedroom while she does her homework or has her in the living room while watching television. Willow is very well behaved except for her passion for stripping wallpaper off the walls and chewing it. Apart from making us worry about whether this would do any harm, it has not been a problem. As the estate agent put it, the house needed 'some modernisation'. However, we are wishing to redecorate both rooms and would appreciate the new wallpaper being left alone.

Answer

Wallpaper can be a great attraction to rabbits. Often it starts with one tiny loose piece and can continue until your wall looks horrendous, with bare bits of plaster and dangling strips of paper. The paper is probably attractive because it is fibrous and chewable. Some animals also seem actually to like the taste of wallpaper paste. Willow has obviously survived her wallpaper chewing, but it is not designed to be eaten and I would not like to state categorically that it has no harmful effects. I suggest that your best course of action is to rabbit-proof the bottom of your walls with strips of Plexiglas. This has the added advantage of preventing accidental scuffing by humans.

Predation

Wild rabbits have many enemies, as do domestic ones. Foxes, stoats, cats and dogs do not naturally distinguish between them: they are all edible. In order to catch a meal a predator has to be stealthy and swift. Your rabbit may be gone before you know it unless you take precautions.

If you are going to give your pet free range of your

garden, then I really do suggest that you are out there to keep an eye on things. If not, then certainly make sure there is plenty of available cover which is not accessible to local cats or other nosy creatures. The best way to ensure this is to protect your rabbit with a well-constructed hutch and run complex. The hutch can either be actually inside the run or attached to one end. Alternatively, you may wish to have a portable run that you can move around your lawn. In this case, do ensure your rabbit is given some shelter in the run. Any wooden structures should be raised off the ground slightly to stop them getting damp. You may need to provide a ramp to assist your rabbit's entry.

Your run should have a wire bottom both to stop your rabbit digging out and to stop a fox digging in. It also needs a lid. This is easily made using a wire-covered wooden frame. Put some hooks on it so you can attach it securely to the main body of the run. At night, when most predators go hunting, it is advisable to lock your rabbit safely in its hutch.

As I am sure you can imagine, losing your rabbit to a predator is extremely distressing and taking precautions is the only way to give yourself peace of mind.

Punishment

Question
If my dog does something wrong I have found that shouting at it or even resorting to tapping it on the nose will teach it how to behave. Is it appropriate to do the same to my rabbit when she does something naughty like chewing wires?

Answer
Punishment is a difficult word. It tends to imply physical force which is really not appropriate. Naturally we all require correction at some point in our lives, but I do

not advocate direct physical punishment for rabbits, or indeed for dogs. Tapping an animal on the nose can mean different things to different people and to different animals. Some dogs, for instance, may retaliate or become fearfully aggressive when your hands are around their faces. Likewise, physically admonishing a rabbit may make it frightened of being approached and set the stage for future fear aggression (see p. 125).

A far better form of correction is to teach the rabbit to associate a particular cue such as 'Thumper, no', with an unpleasant outcome. A spray of water is shocking but harmless and does the trick very nicely (see Attention seeking, p. 96, and Chewing, p. 109). It has the added advantage that it can be done from a distance and so is not directly associated with you. The rabbit will not learn to be frightened of being approached, touched or picked up.

Quantum physics (Schroedinger's Rabbit)

Until you look in the rabbit hutch, you do not know whether or not the rabbit hutch needs cleaning, or whether or not the rabbit is healthy!

Erwin Schroedinger (1887–1961) was an Austrian theorist working in the field of quantum physics. He stated that, in quantum physics, a system exists in all its possible states simultaneously until it is observed to be occupying just one of them.

His famous 'thought experiment' on this topic is known as Schroedinger's Cat and is as follows. Put a cat in a completely sealed box with a sample of radioactive material and a bottle of poison. When sufficient of the radioactive material has decayed it will release a hammer trigger which will in turn break the bottle of poison and so release deadly fumes. Schroedinger suggests that at any point in time the cat will be either alive (because the bottle has not been broken) or dead. The cat is existing in two possible states simultaneously—that is until the box is opened and it is observed which state the cat actually occupies, life or death.

R

Redirected aggression

Redirected aggression refers to aggression which is directed at an object or animal other than the real focus of aggression. It is something we all do. For example, if someone at work has made you angry, you may not be able to deal with it directly, but are irritable with your family instead when you get home. I tend to get very angry with objects such as photocopiers which decide not to work properly when the real source of annoyance may be the fact that I just had a particularly difficult student to deal with, for instance.

Animals, too, redirect their aggression to the nearest available object or animal. The original source of aggression may be something that has angered them or frightened them. Branston (see Learnt aggression, p. 148) occasionally showed some aggression to his cage mate, Pickle, when his owner came to take him out of his hutch. Because Branston could not get rid of the source of his fear (his owners in this case), he became frustrated and took his frustration out on Pickle, who was the nearest available being.

Question
I have a house rabbit, Bambi, who is a great character but does get the sulks. She loves her cuddles and her food and generally is a pleasure to have around. But she is

really quite demanding. While I love to give her cuddles, it is not always convenient. If I put her down before she wishes, or simply say 'Not now, Bambi,' she will often go straight to her toy, a set of wooden keys, and proceed to throw them about. Usually when I come down in the morning, I feed her first thing. If for some reason I do not, perhaps the telephone rings or my daughter or husband needs me, then Bambi has a real tantrum. She grabs the wire side of her kennel and shakes it. Is this really what it seems? It is very reminiscent of the 'terrible twos' I went through with my daughter a decade ago.

Answer

It certainly appears that Bambi is a rabbit who knows exactly what she wants and gets very annoyed, or as you put it, sulky, when the world does not go according to her plan. She is indeed taking her frustration out on her toys and kennel. This can certainly be classified as redirected aggression. Your analogy to the 'terrible twos' is very apt, for that is when human children start to learn that others do not always do exactly what they themselves would like, when they would like.

Relationships

We have seen in this book that rabbits are social animals who can recognise, and form relationships with, individuals of their own and other species and can become quite attached. Being social animals, they like company and will often form a particular relationship to a specific individual. For example, your own rabbit may follow you around the house or garden. It gets on with doing its own thing, eating the grass, exploring the room or even resting, but will go with you if you move away.

Humans, too, form relationships with others. We have different relationships with different people, and with our animals, and these differ in quality and depth. We may have colleagues at work, friends with whom we go out for the evening, family members with whom we are more intimate, and pets. The relationships we have with our pets can be very important to us. Pets can give us emotional support which we may not always be able to receive from other people. They give us what is known as 'unconditional love': they are always pleased to see us, no matter what we look like or how we feel or what we are doing, so long as it is nothing nasty. My dog, for instance, would probably prefer me to take him for a walk right now, but he seems quite content to lie at my feet as I type this. From my point of view this is a very rewarding behaviour of his, which I can call 'devotion'.

All sorts of pets can give us these feelings of being loved, acting as an emotional support. However, research suggests that we tend to form more intense relationships with animals with which we can communicate better, generally social animals with fairly complex visual communication systems, such as dogs, cats, horses and rabbits.

Having a good relationship with an animal has been shown to have health benefits too. Stroking animals which we perceive to be friendly can lower our blood pressure and reduce feelings of stress. Owning pets can help us feel less lonely. This aspect of animals is being used by several charities, such as Pets As Therapy (PAT) and Children in Hospital Pet Therapy Association (CHATA). These groups take good-tempered, calm animals to visit people in care, such as elderly people in residential homes and children in hospital, to give them the pleasure of interacting with an animal. Rabbits can play a positive part for the wider community too. If you are interested in finding out more about these activities, then please contact SCAS (the Society for Companion Animal Studies) whose address is among the useful contacts at the back of this book.

S

Scraping

Question
Earlier this year we decided to get a pet rabbit and got a
pretty little Lop which we have named Hannah. We
obtained her in February and felt it was too cold to put
her outside, so we made her a portable hutch and run
which she had in the garage. Now that the weather is
warmer we have put this out on the lawn for her. She
seems to really enjoy herself, nibbling away, running in
and out of her hutch and lying in the sun, soaking up the
rays, lucky creature. My husband is not enjoying life quite
so much. He is not a man who wants a show garden full
of flowers—tricky with two children and a dog as well—
but he has always been pleased to have a good, green
lawn. Indeed, the reason we have a dog and not a bitch
is that female dog urine tends to make brown patches
on the grass. My husband was rather looking forward to
Hannah 'helping' him with the garden, a bit of natural
mowing and fertilisation, plus being able to use the dirty
newspaper and straw from her hutch in the compost. All
of this she does, but she also scrapes bald patches on the
lawn. Help! My husband is horrified and mutters words
like 'stewpot' under his breath. I should add in his defence
that he has planted a patch of carrots in his flower bed
just for her delectation.

Answer

Oh dear, I can hear the mutterings from here. I am sure there are many readers who sympathise with your husband, especially those whose garden is visited by wild rabbits. It is a good job our pet rabbits have so many endearing qualities to outweigh their misdemeanours. In fact, this problem of lawn damage can be solved quite simply. Hannah is scraping for one or more of several reasons. She may be foraging for tasty young roots, contemplating digging a burrow, or even a nest stop if she has not been spayed, or she is feeling the warmth of the sun and is attempting to fashion a shallow hollow of cool bare earth. You do not say how large or deep these scrapes are, but that would give you an idea of the motivation behind her behaviour. Simply cover the bottom of her run with chicken wire or, if she has small paws, with 1.5–2 cm (½–¾ in) wire mesh. This will allow the grass to grow through, but will stop her excavations. You may wish to provide her with a digging pit (see Digging, p. 115, and Warrens, p. 190), a litter tray filled with cool earth or some clay pipes in which she can lie (see Agoraphobia, p. 90, and Enrichment, p. 119).

Scratching

Rabbits scratch in order to rid themselves of irritating itches and remove dead skin and fur and entangled bits of vegetation. They use their hind limbs to scrabble through their fur with their sharp claws, often at speed and seemingly perilously close to their eyes. If your rabbit seems to be scratching persistently, perhaps even to the point of causing a bald patch, then please take it to the veterinary surgeon. It is likely to be an infestation of some external parasite such as fleas, mites or even lice. Do not be embarrassed about the fact that your rabbit has picked up some such beast; it is easily done even by the best-kept animals. They can pick them up from their surroundings—perhaps the louse dropped off a hedgehog which passed by the night before or fleas fell from a neighbouring cat. It is easy enough to get rid of them and the vet will be able to advise you. The important thing is to be aware of your rabbit's habits and to notice when anything is amiss.

Solitary living
Many pet rabbits are kept as single animals. Indeed, the British Rabbit Council advises this is the way they should be kept. This advice is, however, somewhat out of date; it is also really tailored to those breeders of show rabbits who have several rabbits in rows of hutches. In these cases the prime concern is the rabbit's appearance and there is the worry that rabbits kept together may damage themselves. As we have seen in this book, that is not the case if they are kept properly (see Introductions, p. 140, and Territorial aggression, p. 178). On the contrary, I would argue that keeping a social animal by itself is, potentially, an issue of welfare concern. It is fine to have a single rabbit just as long as you are prepared to give it the time and attention it requires for a happy life. Rabbits are social animals and need companionship. This is just as true whether the rabbit lives in the house, in a hutch or hutch and run in the garden, in a breeder's shed, in a laboratory or in a zoo.

With respect to the pet rabbit, it is not always convenient for us humans to provide this companionship, particularly if the rabbit is in the garden. We sometimes really cannot be bothered to do much more than run to the bottom of the garden in wet weather, quickly fill up the food and water bowl and dash indoors again. Many rabbits are virtually ignored from one day to the next, perhaps only seeing a glimpse of a human for one or two minutes in every 1440, particularly all through the bad weather of autumn, winter and spring. In the summer, there are other things to take our attention away from the rabbit, and we really will give a good cuddle tomorrow, but today . . . Where children are concerned the situation may be no better. A child's interest in the rabbit one summer often wanes and never really comes back again. This means the once loved pet is abandoned to near solitary confinement, for years on end perhaps, until it dies or is lucky enough to go to a more caring home. Pets are not toys or convenience items we can pick up only when we feel like it. They are living, sentient creatures.

The situation is not always a lot better for house rabbits. It may be more convenient to have your rabbit in the house. You do not have to get wet to feed it if it is raining. But sometimes the rabbit may spend long periods in its indoor kennel because the owner is at work all day, and has to dash in and out again because of the recent increase in their social life. It can be just as lonely indoors as outside.

The public does not often think of rabbits having a welfare problem. Yet thousands are given to rescue associations for rehoming, often because the child for whom the pet was bought is no longer interested in keeping it and the parents do not wish to take on the responsibility. I am not sure what sort of moral lesson this teaches a child—that it is all right to discard a living thing simply because it bores you? Approximately two out of every 100 rabbits bought as pets are given to rescue societies, while many more are passed on to friends or rehomed via the local paper or euthanised. Thousands of rabbits die of what is to all intents and purposes neglect, from some preventable condition such as fly strike, obesity or teeth malocclusion. We need to be aware that it is up to us and us alone to provide our rabbits with all they need for their physical and psychological health, and that includes companionship.

T

Teeth
See Anorexia, p. 92.

Territorial aggression
Rabbits, particularly males, show territorial behaviours such as scent-marking. They can also be aggressive if they think their territory is being invaded. Females, too, can be quite aggressive over territory during the breeding season. In both sexes this behaviour is more likely if the rabbit is not neutered (see Neutering, p. 159). While it can be directed towards humans, more often a cage mate of the same sex is the target.

Territorial aggression can be prevented by neutering your rabbits and, just as importantly, giving them sufficient space, with places to get away from each other such as clay pipes and/or two small hutches in the run instead of one. When animals, including humans, are crowded, space or territory becomes more valuable. As a consequence the probability of aggression over what little there is is also likely to increase.

Trancing

Question
Recently I have been told that my rabbit may not like being turned over on his back and having his tummy tickled. Is this right? He lies so still I have assumed he is relaxed and happy. I cannot really believe that he is not happy, as he sometimes flops over on his back of his own accord.

Answer
I am sorry to say that what you have recently heard is likely to be correct. It is a commonly held belief that rabbits which are turned over on their backs are relaxed and happy. In fact, the opposite is true.

When turned on its back a rabbit may struggle initially but soon the muscles relax and the animal enters an apparent trance-like state, in which the only movement is an occasional quivering of one or both hind limbs. Loss of this state occurs as rapidly as it is attained, with a characteristic sudden righting reflex and forward movement. If restraint is continued at this point the animal will struggle and may become aggressive.

The popular explanation, based upon what we know of dog and cat behaviour, is that the rabbit is in a state of 'total bliss'; the change to activity is regarded as anomalous. We should remember, though, that a rabbit is neither a cat nor a dog, but a prey animal. If we look at the behaviour from that point of view we arrive at a completely different and more coherent interpretation.

When seized by a predator many prey species freeze. In the case of the rabbit, it lays its ears flat, partially or fully closes its eyes and enters a state of catalepsy. This immobility increases the probability of the individual escaping uninjured, or only slightly injured, through its resemblance to a successfully killed prey item. The predator then relaxes its hold in order to manipulate the prey

Baby rabbits learn not to become prey items.

into a position where it can be more easily swallowed. The change in grip stimulates the flight response in the rabbit as described above. If thwarted, the flight behaviour switches to fight, a last attempt to escape death. Throughout, the rabbit is conscious and well aware of its situation, just waiting for the split second when it can make a bid for freedom.

What seems a bit strange is that you do not feel the rabbit's heart pounding or much stiffness in its muscles when you hold it upside down, so the rabbit appears relaxed. Scientists have shown that stress can have all sorts of different effects, which can relate to the type of stressor and the response of the particular species. If you are a rabbit trying to imitate a freshly killed animal, a low heart rate and relaxed body tone are adaptive. Researchers studying chickens, which show a similar 'freeze' response, have found that it takes several minutes for the chicken's heart rate to return to normal once the source of stress has been removed.

You also point out that your rabbit voluntarily flops over on his back when at ease. That is quite common behaviour, but completely different from being turned over. I and some colleagues are currently looking at this phenonomen of trancing in rabbits to provide scientific data on what actually happens to a rabbit's heart rate when it is turned upside down and after it is allowed to right itself. Until then I strongly suggest we assume they are similar to other prey species and only put them into a trance state when we need to examine them for their weekly health check, to clip their nails or to determine whether they are male or female.

Trick training

Trick training is really the same as command training and works on the principle technically known as operant learning. That is, the animal learns that if it behaves in a certain way it will obtain something pleasant. This may be a reward such as a treat, a stroke, or access to somewhere it wishes to go. The animal operates the environment to its own advantage. We have already discussed how to teach the rabbit to understand the word 'No', by teaching it that if it stops whatever it is doing it will avoid something unpleasant, and thus obtain something pleasant (see Attention seeking, p. 96). This is an application of operant learning.

Rabbits can also learn tricks. For example, if you wish to teach your rabbit to sit up on command, hold a piece of food above its nose so that it has to reach up to get to it. As it gets up on its hind legs say 'Sit up' and immediately give the rabbit the titbit. Repeat this several times until your rabbit starts to get on its hind legs as you begin to move the food towards it. It is now showing you that it has understood what it has to do in order to obtain the food. Next, try using just the hand signal and the command 'Sit up', then give the food from your other hand. Your rabbit will soon beg on command.

Teaching your rabbit to go into a carrying basket on command will make trips to the veterinary surgery much less traumatic. First get the rabbit used to the basket. Put the basket on its side and place some tasty food inside. Once the rabbit is happy to hop in and out, turn the basket the right way up and entice your rabbit inside. As it gets in say 'Basket.' Repeat the exercise as with the sit up command until the rabbit will go in on cue. Then try saying it when the rabbit is a little further from the basket and get it to follow you to the basket and get in. Your rabbit will soon rush to his basket for his treat. Obviously you can do the same to teach your rabbit to go into his hutch or kennel on command, perhaps using a word such as 'Bedtime'.

If you have a house rabbit, or indeed any rabbit, it can be useful to teach it to walk on a lead. You could then take it for walks around the garden or elsewhere. Special rabbit harnesses and leads can be bought in good pet shops. First allow your rabbit to sniff the harness while you hold it next to him, talking to him quietly. Then, as you offer a nice titbit, gently lay the harness on the rabbit's back so it can get used to the weight. Start by only putting the harness there for a second or two and gradually build up the time it is resting on its back. Once the rabbit is happy with that, put the harness on properly, always with some tempting morsel to keep your rabbit occupied. When the harness and lead are on, let the rabbit trail the lead around as it hops around the room. Once it seems to be ignoring the lead, pick up the handle and walk a step or two away from the rabbit. Entice the rabbit to follow you, perhaps using a command such as 'walkies' in a friendly voice. Do not put any tension on the lead, which would frighten the rabbit and make it pull away. You will soon have your rabbit happily hopping on a lead beside you—though at his or her pace, not yours.

A good word to teach your rabbit is 'Danger' or 'Duck'. This is very useful if your rabbit is out and about and you notice a potential danger like a cat that has just entered your garden, or you want it to move when you are carrying a dish of hot food. Say 'Danger' and immediately afterwards thump your food hard on the ground—the rabbit's own danger signal. Your rabbit will stop, and then run for its home hutch or indoor kennel.

Like dogs and children, rabbits can learn the wrong behaviour just as easily as they can the right. We have already heard of the exploits of Tussle and Mozart (see Attention seeking, p. 96).

Question

I have a rabbit called Budge with whom I share my home. He is so called because it seems I am perpetually budging him out of the way. Perhaps I should have named him Won't Budge. My problem with Budge is that he is a downright thief. He only steals food—any food, even food he does not actually want to eat. Toast off my breakfast plate, bits of ham, etc. He even steals hot food such as potatoes, though he does tend to drop these pretty quickly. Obviously I try not to give him the opportunity, but if I leave the table, say, to answer the phone, he is up on the chair in a trice and, whoosh, something is off the plate. I am rather wary of eating pizza since the incident when I had to get tomato stains out of the carpet. He had left a trail as he had dragged the pizza slice upside down across the room. At first I thought his behaviour was quite funny, and I suppose I did not help matters by occasionally giving him some tasty bits of food, if I had a salad, for instance. It is still rather amusing I admit, but it is rather like having a naughty dog around the home instead of a well-behaved house rabbit!

Answer

You have certainly got a rabbit with an eye for the golden opportunity. As you have rightly indicated, Budge learnt early on that food at the table could be a source of goodies. The goodies in question are not always edible, but certain to get a response from you. That in itself is obviously reward enough. What you have is a case of learnt attention seeking. I suggest you teach Budge the 'No' word (see Attention seeking, p. 96). Then set up some pretend meals and move away from the table. As Budge heads towards the chair, say 'Budge, no.' If you do not get the required response, reinforce your request with a quick spray of water. You may have to do this sneakily from behind the door, if he is to learn that stealing is a no-no whether or not you are in the room. Good luck.

U

Urine

Keeping an eye on your rabbit's urine may not sound the most pleasant of occupations. Just as with faeces, any changes in what comes out of your rabbit may indicate changes inside your rabbit which need the attention of a veterinary surgeon.

Rabbit urine is normally fairly clear and usually yellow. Sometimes it is quite dark and reddish in colour. This may indicate that your rabbit has eaten something quite harmless which has coloured its urine, as cooked beetroot affects ours. Red urine may, however, signify something more sinister, when the redness is actually blood in the urine. This is known as haematuria. It can be caused by the rabbit eating something poisonous or some other medical condition. Common problems are a urinary tract infection (cystitis) or bladder stones, which can affect both males and females and require prompt veterinary care.

Female rabbits which are not spayed may pass red, blood-streaked urine. If your unneutered doe is passing this type of urine, especially if she is older than two or three years, then do take her to your vet. It may be a symptom of cancer or infection of the uterus, and your rabbit may need an operation fast to deal with the problem before it becomes too serious.

It may seem difficult to check a rabbit's urine every day, since they do not usually go in front of you, and they may be doing it in their hutch. But rabbits tend to pass urine and faeces at a single location in their hutch or run. Simply providing them with a cat litter tray with a bit of gravel in the bottom makes it easy to get a sample for the vet to test.

V

Veterinary surgeons
Veterinary surgeons are well-trained professionals who
have spent five years studying at university. Although this
is a long time, it really is not enough to cover every aspect
of animal health for the huge variety of species vets have
to deal with. While most vets will have some basic knowledge of rabbits, particularly with regard to the need for
vaccinations, few have much specialist knowledge. Rabbits
are classed as an exotic species and are not considered in
depth in the veterinary curriculum. Indeed, until recently,
it was thought that little could be done for an ill rabbit.

However, there have been leaps and bounds in rabbit
medicine, matched by an increasing interest from veterinary surgeons in general practice. I have no doubt that this
interest is in part spurred by the recent rise in the popularity of the rabbit as a pet, and one to which owners
become deeply attached and so are willing to do everything possible to keep it in good health.

You may wish to ask your veterinary surgeon if he or
she has a particular interest in rabbits, perhaps attending
'continuing professional development' seminars on the
subject of rabbit health. There are vets with a special interest in the rabbit as a species. The National Rabbit Aid
charity has a list or you may wish to contact the British
Houserabbit Association or the American Houserabbit

Society for details of a specialist veterinary surgeon in your area.

As vets can now do so much more for rabbits, there is the chance that your rabbit will run up quite a bill during its lifetime. It might be sensible to consider taking out health insurance for it. Your veterinary surgeon can advise you on the policies available.

Viral Haemorrhagic Disease (VHD)

VHD is a particularly nasty disease which can rapidly kill a rabbit not protected by vaccination. It is quite new, first reported in 1984 when it affected a group of Angora rabbits imported to China from Germany. In 1986 it was reported in Italy and three years later it had spread across Europe and appeared in southern England. For several years it was considered reasonably rare and any veterinarian who came across a case had to report it to the Ministry of Agriculture. By 1997 it was so entrenched in the British population of wild rabbits it was no longer a notifiable disease.

VHD is a virus carried in the animal's saliva and nasal secretions and is believed to affect only rabbits. It can be transmitted by an infected rabbit coming into contact with another or by being carried accidentally on a person's clothes, on another animal or even on an object such as a water bottle or food bowl. So good hygiene is important if your pet is not to be exposed. It is even more important to have your rabbit vaccinated and to keep up with its booster injections. Depending on the vaccination used, this means a booster once every six or 12 months.

You may think this is all a bit dramatic and overstated, but VHD attacks swiftly and without warning and most rabbits do not survive. The incubation period for the virus can be as long as three days or as short as 16 hours, so your rabbit could appear healthy when you feed him one day but be dead the next. And death from VHD is not pleasant.

If your rabbit contracts VHD, one of three things will

happen. The first is what is known as the 'per-acute' infection. In this case the rabbit will die within a day or two of infection from haemorrhage, suffocation or convulsions. Often there will be a bloody foam coming from its nostrils. The second form is known simply as 'acute'. Again death is the end result, but in this case it will take a few days. The rabbit will appear dull, listless and uninterested in its food. Its breathing will be noisy and forced and again it will suffer an agonising death through haemorrhage, asphyxiation and convulsions. If the rabbit is lucky, usually if it is less than six weeks old or has been inoculated, it will suffer only the mild form, a transient infection which the rabbit usually survives. The rabbit is listless and loses its appetite but recovers after a few days. It may also be vulnerable at this time to secondary infections such as diarrhoea or snuffles. There is usually a bloody discharge around the nostrils and anus.

The answer is simple. Get your rabbit vaccinated, even if it is a house rabbit.

W

Warrens

Under natural conditions rabbits live in a system of burrows they dig underground. Given the opportunity domestic rabbits will also dig extensively. If you let it, your rabbit might tunnel under its run and away and you could lose it. This can be prevented by covering the bottom of its run in chicken wire, which allows the grass to grow through and be neatly nibbled, without letting your rabbit excavate under your lawn. You could provide your rabbit with a 'sand pit' containing a mixture of earth and sand. One 0.6 metres (2 feet) deep and 1.8 to 2 metres (5 or 6 feet) long would give your rabbit a safe place to burrow.

Many years ago I gave two New Zealand White rabbits to the family of my godson. They were known as Sniff and Snuff and had a large hutch and run complex in the garden. The garden was extensive, which was just as well. Over their lifetime they happily constructed an enormous warren. When both the rabbits died, we tried to dig the warren out just to see how big it was. After a day of digging and realising that the burrow system extended for over five metres (16 feet), we said enough was enough and returned indoors to toast Sniff and Snuff's years of work with a well-earned glass of wine.

Water

Rabbits, like all animals, need access to clean, fresh water. The best way of providing this is in a drinking bottle which your rabbit will quickly learn to use. Water in a bowl is likely to be spilt and get dirty. Rabbits do not drink an awful lot, especially if allowed to graze, as they will get much of their requirement from the water in and on fresh grass, but they still need water. Rabbits will drink more if fed on dry food, either concentrates or hay, and also need more water in hot weather. Do change the water daily and ensure the bottle is clean and not growing any algae. You will also need to clean the bottle's nozzle to stop it getting blocked.

In winter you may think that your rabbit is not drinking very much. It may indeed need less water in cool weather, but you should check that it is not because the water has frozen in the bottle or dish.

X, Y, Z

Xenophobia
Literally, xenophobia means a dislike of foreigners. I am not implying that rabbits are nationalistic in that sort of way, but some people think that rabbits do not get on with other species or even rabbits of different breeds.

As we have seen, rabbits can become firm friends with a whole variety of species and can live happily with people, dogs, cats, cavies and other rabbits. However, in all instances they need to be introduced carefully and be given space of their own if life is to be harmonious.

Yelp
Rabbits do, on occasion, yelp or, rather, emit what is more accurately described as an ear-piercing, heart-rending scream. They only do this if they are terrified or in extreme pain, under natural circumstances most often when they have been caught by a predator, maybe to try to scare the predator off. A rabbit being given an injection or euthanised may scream; it is rare but it does happen. This can be very distressing for the owner and it is as well to be aware of the possibility. This is why some veterinarians will suggest that you are not present if your rabbit has to be put to sleep. The injection to put a rabbit to sleep is given straight into the bloodstream, usually directly into the heart or into a vein in the ear. It has an

almost immediate effect and the rabbit does not appear to feel any distress and passes on quietly (see Euthanasia, p. 122).

Zoos

We do not usually think of rabbits as zoo animals, except those kept in children's zoos. A major responsibility of zoos is to educate us about the world we share with animals and to help protect endangered species. While the wild rabbit ancestor of our domestic pets, *Oryctolagus cuniculus*, is not endangered, some of its cousins are not so fortunate. One particularly rare species is the Volcano rabbit, *Romerolagus*. This is a small compact species with a neatly rounded body and petite ears, rather like a Netherland Dwarf. *Romerolagus* lives in the high tablelands near Mexico City and is threatened with extinction. Organisations such as the Jersey Wildlife Preservation Trust have been working closely with rabbit biologists to try to save this species. On behalf of all us rabbit lovers, I wish them every success.

We may think we know a lot about rabbit biology and behaviour and we do know quite a bit about Oryctolagus cuniculus. But we know little about other species, and indeed it would appear we might not even know all the species! In August 1999 it was reported that a new type of rabbit has been found. It is a striped, pretty looking creature and lives in the Annamite Mountains between Laos and Vietnam. It is likely that it is an entirely new species. The natural world will never cease to surprise us.

Appendix One

PLANTS YOUR RABBIT SHOULD NOT EAT

Most good garden centres and nurseries will label plants which are toxic or cause skin allergies. If in doubt, do please contact your veterinary surgeon for advice.

The following list is adapted from the Petplan publication *Top to Tail*, edited by John and Caroline Bower. Where possible I have given the common as well as the Latin name.

CATEGORY A

These plants are poisonous if eaten and will commonly cause severe blistering if they come into contact with skin.

Rhus succedanea	Rhus are part of the Sumach family, poison sumach
Rhus tyhina	
Rhus verniciflua	

CATEGORY B

These plants are toxic if eaten and may cause a skin allergy.

Aconitum	Monkshood
Atropa belladonna	Deadly nightshade
Colchicum	Autumn crocus, meadow saffron, naked ladies

Convallaria majalis	Lily-of-the-valley
Daphne laureola	Spurge laurel
Daphne mezereum	Mesereon, the popular deciduous daphne Other laurel species
Dictamnus albus	Dittany, burning bush
Dieffenbachia	Dumb cane, leopard lily
Digitalis	Foxglove
Gaultheria	Small shrubs with white, pink, purple or blue berries, also known as pernettyas
Gloriosa superba	Glory lily
Hyoscyamus niger	Henbane
Laburnum	Laburnum, golden rain
Lantana	
Nerium oleander	Oleander, rose bay
Phytolacca	Pokeroot, pokeweed
Primula obconica	German primula, poison primula
Ricinus communis	Castor oil plant
Ruta	Rue
Solanum dulcamara	Bittersweet, woody nightshade
Taxus	Yew
Veratrum album	False hellebore
Zantedeschia aethiopica	Arum lily

CATEGORY C

These plants are harmful if eaten and can cause skin allergy.

Aesculus	Horse chestnut
Agrostemma	Corn cockle
Alstroemeria	Peruvian lily
Aquilegia	Columbine

Brugmansia	Angel's trumpets
Caltha	Kingcup, marsh marigold
Caltharanthus roseus	
Cupressocyparis leylandii	Leyland cypress (often used as hedging)
Delphinium	Delphinium
Dendrathema	Formerly classified as chrysanthemums
Echium	Viper's bugloss
Euonymus	Spindle tree
Euphorbia	Spurge
Ficus carica	Fig (both for indoor and outdoor growing)
Fremontodendron	Flannel bush
Hedera	Ivy
Helleborus	All hellebores
Hyacinthoides	Bluebell
Hyacinthus	Hyacinth
Hypericum	St John's Wort
Ipomoea	Morning glory
Iris	Iris
Juniperus sabina	Juniper
Kalmia latifolia	Calico bush, mountain laurel
Ligustrum	Privet
Lobelia spp.	Lobelia
Lupinus	Lupins
Narcissus	Narcissus, daffodils
Ornithogalum	Star-of-Bethlehem
Polygonatum	Solomon's seal
Prunus laurocerasus	Cherry laurel
Rhamnus	Buckthorn
Schefflera	Ivy tree
Thuja	(hedging conifers)
Tulipa	Tulips
Wisteria	Wisteria

If you are in doubt, please do not give a plant, flower or twig to your rabbit. If you think your rabbit has eaten anything poisonous, do not delay but take it straight to your veterinary surgeon.

Appendix Two

HOW TO TEACH YOUR DOG TO LEAVE

Leave means 'Leave it, it is boring. Pay attention to me; I am exciting and rewarding.' As a consequence, 'Leave' is a gently spoken command and the dog is rewarded verbally as well as with food or play.

Remember that the more important what you are asking the dog to leave is to the dog, the greater the payment you will have to offer. Would you leave your pen for someone who said 'Please' and offered you £2.00? Would you leave your car for the same price? I suspect not, but you might for £20,000.

Stage A

Hold a piece of food in the tips of your fingers. As the dog approaches, say 'Leave' gently and close your hand.

As the dog retracts its head, say 'Good. Leave. Take it,' and give the dog the food.

When the dog is clear that it has to move its head away from the food in order to obtain it, then move on to the next stage.

Stage B

Sit in a chair. Hold your right arm, with the food in your fingers, out to the right. As the dog goes to take the food, say 'Leave.' If the dog does not move its head away, close your fingers and repeat the command. When it does move its head away, bring the food back to your lap (crotch), and tell the dog to 'Take it' and give it the food . . . making it come to your lap for the food.

When the dog is clear on this, move on to the next stage.

Stage C

Repeat stage B in terms of holding the food out to your right. Say 'Leave,' and make some distraction to get the dog to look at you, such as scratching the top of your head with your other hand.

When it looks at you, tell it that it is a 'Good dog,' bring the food back to your lap and tell the dog to 'Take it.'

Build up the length of time the dog will look at you to ten seconds. As long as the dog is looking at you, say 'Good dog.' If it looks at the food, repeat the leave command.

When the dog is clear about what it has to do, move on to the next stage.

Stage D

Put some fairly boring object on the floor. As the dog approaches or sniffs it, gently ask it to 'Leave.' As the dog looks at you, say 'Good dog,' and entice it back to you. Then reward it with a piece of food given from your hand in your lap with the take it command. Repeat this exercise with a variety of boring items.

Note: once the dog understands this, it may go and sniff an item and then immediately return to you. If you have *not* said 'Leave,' then do *not* reward the dog but ignore it. We wish the dog to learn that 'Leave' is the cue and that you are in control.

Practise stage D on a variety of items in a variety of places, e.g., ask the dog to 'Leave' as you pass a bush or lamp-post and reward the dog as it looks at you.

Once this is going well, go on to the next stage.

Stage E
Go back to working in a quiet area and repeat stage D, using a variety of more interesting items such as the dog's toys.

Then practise in a variety of different places.

When this is going well, go on to the next stage.

Stage F
Back in your quiet area, start the silly games routine:

The handler keeps the dog's attention using food or toys. The dog should be kept facing the handler, so hold the food or toy in the area of your lap. As long as the dog is concentrating, praise it in a fairly excited voice.

The silly person starts to move about, waving his hands or doing the cancan. Adjust the silly person's level of activity to the dog's response, building it up as the dog responds to the Leave command.

Rule: the silly person is not allowed to say the dog's name or a command such as 'Come.'

If the dog breaks away from the handler, the silly person is to stop immediately and totally ignore the dog (no eye contact), only resuming activity once the handler has the dog back under control.

If the dog looks at the silly person, the handler should say 'Leave' gently and regain its attention, rewarding it verbally, and then keep its attention with the titbits, posting one into the dog's mouth every so often, or letting it mouth the toy.

If the dog breaks away towards the silly person, then lure it back to position using the food or toy and repeating the leave command.

Practise in a variety of areas with a variety of silly games.

You are now ready to introduce your dog to your rabbit.

Appendix Three

HOW TO BUILD A RABBIT RUN

If you provide your rabbit with a run and enrichment (see Enrichment p. 120) you will enable it to get the physical and mental exercise it needs. The run can be either free-standing or attached to the hutch.

Traditionally, such runs are made from timber batten framing and covered with galvanised wire mesh 'chicken wire', as seen in many pet shops. In order to deter predators, it is essential that runs have sufficient weight to hold them down, or that they are pegged to the ground and placed on a level site.

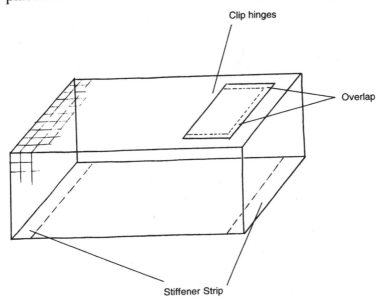

Clip hinges

Overlap

Stiffener Strip

A perfectly good run can be made using welded wire mesh, 'C' clips and a pair of pliers (see diagram). A suitable mesh would be 3×3 cm $\times$ 12 (2×2 in $\times$ 12) gauge or 10 gauge in galvanised finish. This is available in sheet form. The run should be high enough to allow your full-grown rabbit to stretch and large enough to allow it to hop freely. Remember to provide fresh water and food and a sheltered area so that the rabbit can take cover from wind, rain and too much sun. Such runs can be easily dismantled when they need to be moved or stored.

USEFUL ADDRESSES

UNITED KINGDOM

Association of Pet Behaviour Counsellors
PO Box 46, Worcester WR8 9YS.

The Association of Pet Behaviour Counsellors is a national organisation of people specialising in the resolution of behaviour problems. For information about your nearest practitioner, or advice on how to become a behaviour counsellor, please send an A5 SAE.

British Houserabbit Association
PO Box 346, Newcastle Upon Tyne NE99 1FA.

The British Houserabbit Association is a club for rabbit owners of all ages, especially those with a specific interest in having their pet indoors on a full- or part-time basis. For further information, please send an A5 SAE.

British Rabbit Council
Purefoy House, 7 Kirkgate, Newark, Nottinghamshire NG24 1AD.

The British Rabbit Council is the governing body of the rabbit fancy and will provide information on the breeding and exhibition of rabbits. For further information, send an A5 SAE.
   Fur and Feather, the journal of the British Rabbit Council, is published fortnightly and provides advice and infor-

mation on rabbits and other small mammals such as cavies and mice. For subscription details and helpline, please telephone 01473 652789.

National Rabbit Aid
Bristol HQ, 108 Staple Hill Road, Fishponds, Bristol BS16 5AH.

National Rabbit Aid is a charitable organisation which provides advice and care sheets to rabbit owners as well as lists of veterinary surgeons who specialise in rabbit health.

The Rabbit Charity
PO Box 23698, London N8 0WS.

Society for Companion Animal Studies
10b Leny Road, Callander, Scotland FK17 8BA. Tel: 01877 330996.

UNITED STATES OF AMERICA

American Rabbit Breeders Association
1925 Southmain, Box 426, Bloomington, Illinois 61702. Tel: (309) 664 7500.

Houserabbit Society
PO Box 1201, Alamedon, California 94501. Tel: (510) 521 4631.

Delta Society
289 Perimeter Road East, Renton, WA 98055-1329.

Rabbits Only (magazine)
PO Box 207, Holbrook, New York 11741. Tel: (516) 737 0099. Website: www.rabbits.com

FURTHER READING

McBRIDE, A. (1988). *Rabbits and Hares.* London: Whittet Books.

REES, R. (1997). *The Problem with Rabbits.* Neston, Liverpool: Green Fork Publisher.

SANDFORD, J. (1996). *The Domestic Rabbit* (fifth edition). Oxford: Blackwell Sciences.

Index